To Laurie,

May your life be filled
with Faith, hope + Love!

THE GIFT OF LIFE, LOVE, AND HEALING

"God is Love" 1 Jn 4:8

Love,

Mark & Judy

The **Gift** of Life, Love, and Healing

Mark Paul Bishop, M.D.

Mustard Seed Press
Dodgeville, Wisconsin

First printing.

Mustard Seed Press, 502 Lindsey Street, Dodgeville, Wisconsin 53533, 608-935-5799

Book design by Dorie McClelland, Spring Type & Design, St. Paul MN
Printed by Olympic, Minneapolis MN

ISBN 0-9655904-0-2

THIS BOOK IS DEDICATED TO...

My wife, Judy, for her love and faithfulness;

My children, Brad, Brent, and Carrie, for their love and understanding;

My parents, Dr. Paul and Alice Bishop, for their love and my life;

My brothers and their families, Neil and Kathy, Reb, Nancy, Torry and Bryn; Paul Mac; Alan, Cindy, Megan, Anna, and Kendara; Bill, Christy, Brook, and Hannah, for their love and support;

Elva Washington, who called herself "our brown mother," for her faithfulness and prayers;

Joe and Myrl Garvey for their steadfast love, support, and spiritual encouragement;

Tom and Josie Tarnutzer for their love and friendship;

Carl and Pearl George, Judy's mother and dad, for Judy's life;

Judy's brothers and sisters and their families for their love and support;

Pastor Steve and Becky Moltumyer for sharing the Gospel;

The communities, churches, hospitals, clinics, and staff of Haynesville, Louisiana, Sauk Prairie, Wisconsin, Graham, Texas, Dodgeville and Mineral Point, Wisconsin, for their acceptance and loyalty;

My sincere patients for their confidence and loyalty, and for granting me the ultimate privilege of being able to share in their lives;

The University of Wisconsin Hospital and Medical School, and St. Mary's Hospital Medical Center, and their staffs for providing me a medical education;

The doctors, nurses, therapists, and clinical staffs of Graham General Hospital, Harris Hospital, St. Mary's Hospital Medical Center, New Start, Memorial Hospital of Iowa County, The University of Wisconsin Hospitals, and Dayton General Hospital, and The McBride Center for helping us regain our health.

Kathy Westhoff, Donna Thielorn, and the Department of Health Information at Memorial Hospital of Iowa County for their cooperation and patience in the preparation of this manuscript.

My wife, Judy, and Dorie McClelland for their editorial and artistic contributions.

CONTENTS

PHOTOGRAPHS

Introduction

1. HUMP BACK WHALE

And the Lord appointed a great fish to swallow Jonah, and Jonah was in the stomach of the fish three days and three nights. JONAH 1:17 TLB

1 ✦ Introduction

This book was born shortly before Christmas of 1994 when I was taking a personal inventory and counting my personal blessings. At that time I was well, but a few years earlier I had been racked by the pain of a spinal cord injury and left with an unstable spine resulting from an accident. I had undergone personal suffering and misery which had taken me to my knees. In the end, after four extensive back surgeries to relieve the pressure on my spinal cord and stabilize my spine with a five-level spinal fusion, I was on my back. In every sense of the word I was down for the count. I was unable to work, I saw no end to my physical misery, I was financially devastated, I was mentally, emotionally, and spiritually bankrupt.

Only weeks before my scheduled final corrective spinal surgery, I wondered what else could possibly go wrong? In the midst of my own misery I thought I could bear no more. Then, my oldest son Brad, two weeks before his high school graduation, came home with a rash on his legs, a sore throat, and a fever. I hoped it was mono. But when I felt the nodules on his spleen my worst fears were realized. Brad had acute lymphoblastic leukemia—cancer of the bone marrow. When I was in medical

2. Glacier

I went down to the bottoms of the mountains that rise from the ocean floor. I was locked out of life and impris-oned in the land of death. Jonah 2:6 TLB

school this diagnosis carried with it a certain death sentence. Brad was immediately entered into an aggressive chemotherapy protocol.

Within the first week he was in a coma from kidney failure. Within two months he collapsed on the floor in our bedroom in a continuous seizure. He had been unable to swallow due to the severe mouth sores from his chemotherapy which caused him to choke. I tried to support him on the floor and clear his windpipe of the glue-like saliva that filled his throat. He continued to seize and stopped breathing. I started mouth-to-mouth resuscitation and carried his spastic body to the back of our vehicle. I tossed him onto the back seat like a vibrating sack of potatoes; then dove in on top of him to continue mouth-to-mouth resuscitation. My wife, Judy, drove us to our hospital where I again carried his seizing, rigid, bony body into the main trauma emergency room. We were immediately attended by nurses, lab and x-ray technicians and a respiratory therapist. With help supporting his breathing and suctioning his airway free of the goo, we were able to stop his seizing with intravenous medication.

I immediately called his cancer doctor for help! He was gone on vacation and out of town. I called the doctor taking his calls who was very helpful but was equally as perplexed as I by our circumstance. I started to feel real lonely and inadequate so I stopped feeling and continued to expend what energy I had in thinking. Working through the years of my medical training and medical practice I had developed a certain amount of confidence in the science and technology of medicine. But while working at a feverish pace implementing all of the medical, scientific, and technological expertise available, I was taken into a silent vigil of prayer as I had done many times on behalf of my suffering patients. But, I must admit that I had often gone to God in prayer for my own relief and recovery, but had lost my faith that He was actually there for me. If He was there, how could He sit back and allow one calamity after another to occur?

With this anguished, skeptical reasoning in full swing I recalled the parable in the Bible, Luke 7:41, where loans of money were made to two different men. The first man had a loan of $5000. The second man had a loan of $500. Of the two, the most grateful for the eventual forgiveness of the loan would certainly be the man who owed the most—the man who was loaned $5000. At this point I valued my own personal loan at $500. But for my son's survival and recovery I placed the value of that loan for God's intervention to be worth the full $5000. Relating that parable to my desperate situation, I had a renewed faith in the plan and purpose of our circumstance. Could it be that God was allowing such a situation to occur so that we as individuals would be placed in a situation where we experienced both the depth of His grace and love and at the same time would be left with a profound gratitude toward Him? A gratitude so profound that it would have a lasting impact on our lives and on our service to Him.

I was able to get telephone consultation and advice from leukemia experts from all over the country. Aided by a computer search of the medical complications of this type of leukemia and its treatment, it was revealed that Brad had probably suffered a stroke from a blood clot lodged in his brain. After the results of a CAT scan of his head to rule out a brain hemorrhage and a spinal tap to rule out meningitis, the results confirmed at least two clots in his brain. An MRI scan of his brain revealed three areas of brain injury caused by blood clots lodged in his brain. By now his legs were purple from his waist down to his toes. He had nearly lost the circulation to his legs resulting from clots clogging his leg arteries. At the same time he was hemorrhaging into his skin and out of his nose and mouth. Not only had he lost the ability to clot his blood, he had also lost the ability to break down naturally occurring blood clots in his blood stream. This paradoxical condition was specific to his treatment and its effects on his liver where the proteins responsible for blood clot formation and blood clot breakdown are made. One of the areas of his brain injury involved the region of the brain needed for vision. In his now semi-responsive state, he told me he could not see. He was blind! It appeared as though he may lose his legs! Then he lapsed into a coma. He was now out of the Emergency Department and was in our hospital's intensive care unit. He was undoubtedly the sickest person I had ever cared for.

With the help from numerous consultants, a constant vigil by my entire family, continued support and attendance by my co-workers and dedicated nurses, I knelt at his bedside pleading with God for his life. My wife Judy, and my two other children, Brent and Carrie, were stricken by fear and worry. They moped about the ICU room dazed by their terror and disbelief. As I watched his bluish-purple, frail body pulsate with every heart beat, I realized just how fragile life could be. But at the same time I saw how rugged and determined life could be. Contained within his frail, disease ravaged, emaciated and bony discolored body was the strength of Brad's human spirit. A spirit which had the strength and power to not let go of life. A spirit set into motion at creation destined to find a way to survive and live. As a physician I had initiated and implemented all that was known by science and technology to his condition in support of his physical body. What else could be done to support his life? Was there a real substance and foundation for my own faith and prayers?

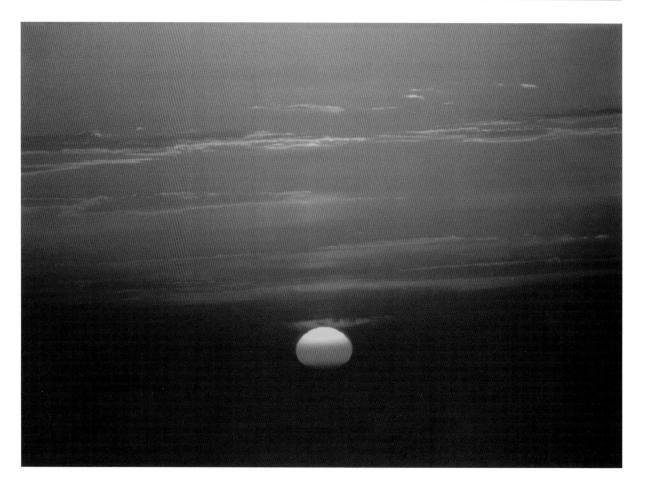

3. LIGHT OUT OF DARKNESS

In the beginning GOD created the heaven and the earth. And God said, "Let there be light:" and there was light. And God saw the light, that it was good: And God divided the light from the darkness...and the evening and the morning were the first day. GENESIS 1:1,3-5 KJV

2 ◆ The Foundation of My Faith

Eighteen years ago, in the back room of a hospital, I had been on my knees to ask God into my life by accepting Christ as my personal Savior. Pastor Steve, a friend and patient of mine, had sensed my searching for the answer to man's inner struggle for life's purpose, meaning, worth, joy, acceptance, and love. Not long after I completed my medical training, I discovered an affliction in my patients and then in myself for which medicine had no answer. That just as the physical body needs oxygen, nutrition and exercise to stay healthy, the soul and spirit of man needs the nurturance and relationship with God to stay healthy. That every human seeks a sense of personal worth, and validation of meaning and purpose in life. Simply stated, every human needs and seeks the affirmation of unconditional love and acceptance from God. But we humans, in our appraisal of ourselves often conclude, as a result of our own thoughts and actions, that either we are unacceptable to God or we don't need God. But, we all have a problem with sin and we know it. It is sin that caused our separation from God in the beginning through the disobedience of Adam. That single act of defiance and disobedience by

4. Firmament

And God said, "Let there be a firmament in the midst of the waters and let it divide the waters from the waters"…And God called the firmament Heaven. And the evening and the morning were the second day.
Genesis 1:6,8 KJV

Adam continues to separate us from God during our own lives. What are we to do? God has provided us as individuals a way to resolve our sin problem and become reunited with Him. His plan for accomplishing this reunion is carried out through the life, death, and resurrection of His Son, Jesus. His life shows us love in action. His death provides a mechanism for resolving our sins—when we accept the death of Christ as payment for our sins God freely wipes our slate clean. In God's eyes we are then as guiltless, blameless and perfect as Christ himself. Boy, does that take faith! Yes, and our amount of faith is what pleases God and makes us acceptable to Him. But also, after we accept Christ as our bridge to God, we are also given the free gift of eternal life in heaven. This is demonstrated by the resurrection of Christ himself after His crucifixion. Just as He went to be in heaven with God, so too will we be in heaven with God. After death, our transformed physical bodies will some day meet our already perfected spirits in heaven. God's plan for His faithful is no less complete than His plan for His Son. So, what I realized, and what I experienced at my own salvation when I said the sinner's prayer with Pastor Steve, was love, acceptance, meaning, purpose, and the security of being in the will of the creator of my life—God. I found security in knowing that I fit into the scheme of life and the world. I also found security in the fact that my life will go on into eternity. When God asks me, "why should I accept or allow you into my home in heaven?" I can boldly give the one and only correct answer—"because I have accepted your Son, Christ, as my Savior." Well, that sounds awful narrow minded! But, it is indeed the foundation of my faith. As Christ Himself said—

Heaven can be entered only through the narrow gate! The highway to hell is broad, and its gate is wide enough for all the multitudes who choose its easy way. But the gateway to life is small, and the road narrow and only a few will ever find it. MATTHEW 7:13-14 TLB

But what does all this have to do with Brad's critical condition? There are many marvelous and wondrous interactions between the spirit and soul of people and their physical body. When a person's spirit is in harmony with God's Spirit, the opening is there for His direct and personal intervention.

I must admit that I had frequently asked God for the evidence of His presence in my life. I am sure based on my skepticism, that I doubted most of His direct answers. After all, how does

5. LAND

And God said, "Let the waters under the heavens be gathered together unto one place, and let the dry land appear." And the evening then the morning was the third day. GENESIS 1:9, 13 KJV

one separate that happening or circumstance derived from personal will, effort, or mere chance from a direct intervention from God? I had no appreciation for the depth of wisdom or insight of the following message in which to perceive the circumstances of life. In short, I had little faith.

There is no such thing as chance, and what we regard as blind circumstance actually stems from the deepest source of all.
                                        –Friedrick VonSchiller

For my entire Christian life I had been perplexed and confused by attempting to separate the works of man and probability of chance from that of God. I often pleaded with God to show me a situation with 100% certainty, no doubts, ifs, ands or buts about it, that He was indeed there, and that when He did, I would announce His presence to everyone.

Well, in order to show me His presence, He had to allow a situation to develop which was 100% totally beyond my own personal control. And there I was in the battle of my life, literally for the life of my son, with all of my personal strengths and reserves expended and exhausted.

My mind raced through my life's experiences searching for a similar encounter with desperation. I recalled the dire circumstance faced by Jonah as he faced with desperation an eminent life and death situation. I recalled his personal narration of his circumstance and decided to apply his successful reasoning and action to my own state of personal desperation. At that point I drew my personal line in the sand and like Jonah committed myself to the following reasoning, conclusions and personal commitments.

Then Jonah prayed to the Lord his God from inside the fish:
"In my great trouble I cried to the Lord and He answered me, from the depths of death I called, and the Lord, You heard me! You threw me into the ocean depths, I sank down into the floods of waters and was covered by your wild and stormy waves. Then I said, 'Oh Lord, you have rejected me and cast me away. How shall I ever again see Your Holy Temple?'

"I sank beneath the waves, and death was very near. The waters closed above me, the seaweed wrapped itself around my head. I went down to the bottoms of the mountains that rise from off the ocean floor. I was locked out of life and imprisoned in the land of death. But, Oh Lord My God, You have snatched me from the yawning jaws of death!

"When I had lost all hope, I turned my thoughts once more to the Lord. In my earnestness I went

6. SUN   7. MOON

And God said, "Let there be light in the firmament of the heavens to divide the day from the night; and let them be for signs, and for seasons, and for days, and years;"...And the evening and the morning was the fourth day. GENESIS 1:14,19 KJV

to You in Your Heavenly Temple. (Those who worship false gods have turned their backs on all the mercies waiting for them from the Lord!)

"I will never worship anyone but You! For how can I thank you enough for all You have done? I will surely fulfill my promises. For my deliverance comes from the Lord alone." And the Lord ordered the fish to spit up Jonah on the beach, and it did. JONAH 2:5-9 TLB

As I clung to Brad's frail, discolored body in the intensive care unit for the next few hours, all I could do was hope and pray for the presence of God's Spirit to sustain Brad's life. Neither Brad's nor my own body had enough personal strength left to sustain a fight for life. So, by circumstance I was forced to play the only card I had left in my hand—the hope that the power and presence of God's Spirit would sustain life.

As I watched Brad's emaciated body pulsate with each heart beat, I wondered, "Where is his strength coming from? Where does this drive for life originate?" If the spirit of man is a mere manifestation of the biology of his brain and body, then Brad's spirit would not survive or sustain him. For in the circumstance of his illness, Brad's brain and body were badly diseased and injured. Then I realized proof positive, 100% certain, no

ifs, ands, or buts about it, God's actual presence was real. It was God's Spirit that refused to depart Brad's ravaged body.

It was God's Spirit in me that was also sustaining me beyond my own physical capabilities. I realized what Paul had meant when he delighted in his own weakness. For as Paul reasoned, when we are weak, it shows how strong God is. But the only way I as an individual could ever come to believe the essence of this spiritual truth was to live it. I had to experience personal weakness and emptiness in order to realize the greatness of God. In these early morning hours in the ICU, God revealed Himself to me as the force and power behind life itself. He revealed Himself to me as a personal God with me through all things. That His Spirit in me as the Holy Spirit indwelling in me from my salvation was not merely abstract, or religious rhetoric, but was really the truth.

When Brad was a child, I explained to him the necessity for his own personal salvation. After all, Christ in fact commands us to come to Him as a little child. So Brad knew full well as a child that he needed God. I could remember in the bedroom on our knees at the bedside, Brad accepting Christ as his Savior. (I was witness to the same event in Brent and Carrie's lives.) He, too, had the presence of the Holy Spirit within

8. BLUE HERON   9. TROUT   10. GEESE FLYING

And God said, "Let the waters bring forth abundantly the moving creatures that hath life, and fowl that may fly above the earth in the open firmament of heaven."...And the evening and the morning were the fifth day. GENESIS 1:20,23 KJV

him. So I began to ask God through the activation of His Holy Spirit in Brad not to let go of him. As I watched each heart beat heave in his chest I was assured that Brad was in God's hands, not mine, and not man's.

Oh! Believe me, I made vows and promises, I swore up and down to this and that to make a deal with God to save Brad. But I realized that if He decided to take Brad, that my son would be in perfect health and harmony in God's hands. This reality created an assurance and a calm in the midst of the most terrible storm I ever encountered. But, I couldn't accept this as God's Will—although I had observed many people of God, more faithful and more courageous than I, accept just that destiny in their own lives. But God's Spirit in me was persuading me to hang on to life, faith, hope, and God's love.

Realizing my own state of physical, emotional, and spiritual weakness I asked God, through His Holy Spirit in me, to provide me with an extra measure of will, determination, faith, and hope. These very qualities had always come naturally to me, so I never knew if they were from my natural person or from God. But now realizing that my natural qualities were spent and exhausted, I knew that if these qualities were revived they would undoubtedly have come from outside of my nat-

ural person. Since Brad was in a coma, brain and body diseased and injured, if these qualities could sustain him, they too, would have to come from an outside source. With each continued heart beat I observed my strength of faith, hope, and love being renewed. I clung tightly to Brad in hopes that some of my strength would pass over to him.

That crisis was met with the power of God's presence and strength. I saw first hand evidence of a force and power outside of ourselves called into the presence of a dire situation by love, faith, and hope. God's Holy Spirit does indeed reside in His faithful. God is faithful to those who love Him and have faith in Him. Christ is that catalyst who by God's plan comes to each individual as a person. The Person of Christ is the bridge between God and us as individuals. It is through Christ, that we come to know God. Look what Christ Himself said—

I AM the agent of my Father in everything; and no one can really know the Son except the Father—and no one really knows the Father except the Son and those to whom the Son chooses to reveal Him. LUKE 10: 22 TLB

Brad began to regain his vision on the third day after his strokes. He went on, over the next three years, to suffer nearly every complication

11. CATTLE

12. INSECT

13. FROG

14. BADGER

And God said, "Let the earth bring forth the living creatures after his kind, cattle, and creeping things, and beasts of the earth after his kind." GENESIS 1:24 KJV

Then God said, "Let Us make man in Our image, according to Our likeness; and let them rule over the fish of the sea and over the birds of the sky and over the cattle and over all the earth, and over every creeping thing that creeps on the earth"....And the evening the the morning were the sixth day. GENESIS 1:26 KJV

known to his illness and its treatment. He was hospitalized some seventeen times in the battle for his life, enduring bleeding ulcers, life threatening infections, the chronic pain of nerve damage from his chemotherapy, the acute and chronic pain of shingles, and experienced his own degree of emotional and spiritual pain, suffering, and anguish.

During these three years, I had my own personal struggles through two more major operations. One for decompressing my spinal cord and spinal nerves. And a second, for stabilizing five levels of unstable vertebrae with steel rods. I was taken on many occasions to my absolute limits of tolerance of pain and addiction to pain medication in order to survive my misery. Judy, Brent, and Carrie lived like nomads from one room to another, one hospital to another, one crisis to another. There was absolutely no normalcy in our lives. My faith was sustained by the love of my wife Judy, and my ever faithful family. God knew I had little faith of my own left to go on. We all were sustained by the love and prayers of our many family members, friends, and my many loyal and faithful dear patients.

Through the marvels of modern medicine and professional help, the health of my body, emotions, and spirit were all rehabilitated and strengthened. I experienced a revived and vital

faith in the reality of God's presence and power. I had to lose a lot of things before I could see what was important. I had to experience total emptiness before I could begin to be filled with God.

Just as if someone had planned it, my state of renewed health occurred at the same time Brad completed his horrendous course of chemotherapy. He, too, was left physically, emotionally, and spiritually devastated. He, too, had become addicted to pain medication which he took constantly for the pain of his damaged nerves resulting from his many complications.

Additionally, there was a legitimate concern from his doctors that Brad's strokes and radiation therapy to his brain had left him brain-damaged. These concerns were discussed with me in private so as not to affect Brad emotionally. I listened respectfully and then proceeded not to follow through with the doctor's plan of advising Brad to modify and change his life's goals. For I knew he had something in him stronger than any obstacle he would confront in this life and in this world. In fact, he went on to become an honor student majoring in mechanical engineering. He is experiencing his heart's desire of working with engines.

I had seen it, and read about it, and studied it for years, but now I was experiencing it—when a devastating illness occurs in a family the whole

15. WATERFALL

Thus the haven and the earth were finished, and all the host of them. And on the seventh day God rested from all His work which He had made. GENESIS 2:1,2 KJV

family gets sick. We all needed help getting back on track. Just as if we had all been through a war, we were all left shell-shocked. I will never forget how terrible I felt when I looked into the blank, emotionless apathetic eyes of depression worn by Judy, Brad, Brent, Carrie, and yes, myself. So much stress, anxiety, worry, pain, and suffering caused us all to lose our perspectives on life. Along the road to recovery our whole family received supportive physical, emotional and spiritual help.

❊

This brings me to why I wrote this book. At times I have failed, but I have honestly and sincerely tried to be true to my own mission in life; which I stated on my application to medical school—"I want to exhaust my human potential in the service to my fellow man." As I was contemplating my blessings in that Fall of 1994, I wanted to share with others what God had done for my family and myself. After all, we have all regained our health. We have experienced a sense of joy to the extent I previously thought unimaginable. I have been blessed with a faith that is real. I have never been more assured and confident of the presence of God in the drama of

human life. I chose to write this book as a means of sharing with others what I have learned and experienced about love, life and healing. In the process of regaining my perspectives on life, I looked not only to the inside, but also to what was on the outside. I began to see evidence upon which to base my faith in all things around me. My desire is to share the simplicity of God with those who are in need and who are searching. I intend to show the person in need how to establish a personal faith and develop a personal relationship with God through Christ.

My hope is to demonstrate to others the simple principles of God. I hope that others can make application of these simple gifts and provisions of God in their time of need. They give us life and sustain us through all of the triumphs as well as the tragedies in life. Through the operation of faith, hope, and love, we can experience physical healing, as well as the inner spiritual healing which leads to joy, peace, patience, kindness, goodness, faithfulness, gentleness, and self control—these are the fruits of the Holy Spirit and truly do become a reality to those who seek after God's Will for their lives.

The ability to experience these fruits starts with our personal acceptance of Christ as our Lord and Savior. He is our most cherished gift

16. THE TRINITY – THE LIGHT BREAKS THROUGH

But ye shall receive power after that the Holy Ghost is come upon you; and ye shall be witnesses unto Me, both in Jerusalem, and in all Judea, and in Samaria, and unto the uttermost parts of the earth. ACTS 1:8 KJV

from God. God sent Him to us on the first Christmas. My fundamental intent is to merely relate to others what Christ, and therefore Christmas, means to me. Its meaning is like life—it is both simple and profound. But I am convinced that God intends for each of us as individuals to see His Gift of Christ for what simple and profound realities it has for our lives. Christ is the substance of all things seen and unseen—I hope you see Him for yourself.

On my road to reason and recovery I began to simply use my life's experiences to reconstruct the meaning of life. My process of reconstruction began with the simple observations of the fundamentals of life in nature. These observations led me to consider the essence of life, which is creation. The consideration of creation naturally led me to the foundation of creation.

My pursuit led me to find the character, the person, and the power of the Creator. It led me to God. It led me to reconsider the Creator's plan for man and for me. I was led to a spiritual healing by looking at the intricate, engineering marvel of an insect, by looking at the intricate beauty and diversity of a wild flower, by looking at those life forms all around me.

I found my physical healing to be fully experienced and appreciated only after my spiritual

healing was complete. I would like to share with you my journey to the truth, meaning, purpose, rhyme, and reason to life. In so doing, my hope is that others may in some way find for themselves the source of my healing and personal joy for living. My hope is that the reader will find and see that God reveals Himself to us through His Word and creation but relates to us through His Son. The object of our faith and worship should not be that which is created, but should be the Creator.

The ultimate and simplistic source of life, love and healing is provided to us by God through our relationship with Christ. My hope is that the reader personally experience the power and the magnitude of the good news of Christ or the Gospel of Christ—that Christ is God's provision to man through His life, death, and resurrection for the personal experience and reality of love, forgiveness, and eternal life.

And please remember that no matter how difficult life may be or become, those burdens which are your's to carry will never completely overpower you. God has promised never to over burden one of His faithful. If your's seems greater than mine or those around you, it is only because God has given you a greater degree of strength.

No matter how tempting it may be in times

of distress and duress to give up, God will provide you with the strength to endure or with an escape route so that you will not be over powered by a situation or circumstance. Just when I thought He had forgotten my family and me, I began to look around and see that the evidence of His presence was everywhere. It is my final hope that the reader come to believe and have faith in this promise and provision for yourself as I did for myself; and that you may also be reassured of His presence and provision by seeing the majesty of His creation around you.

Many others have faced exactly the same problems before you. An no temptation is irresistible. You can trust God to keep the temptation from becoming so strong that you can't stand up against it, for He has promised and will do what He says. He will show you how to escape temptations power so that you can bear up patiently against it. I CORINTHIANS 10:13

MY FAMILY: I AM THANKFUL FOR OUR LIFE, LOVE, AND HEALTH. AT OUR HOME IN DODGEVILLE, WISCONSIN. DR. MARK AND JUDY (FRONT), BRAD, BRENT, AND CARRIE (BACK, LEFT TO RIGHT). Berard Photography.

Relationships

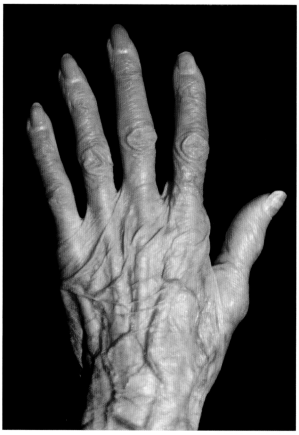

17. Leaf   18. Rose's Hand

And God saw everything that He had made, and behold, it was very good. Genesis 1:31 NAS

3 ✦ Mankind's Relationship with Creation

The essence of life is creation. Creation is life. It is with a sense of awesome reverence that we should view life. For our very own lives have been a gift of creation by the hand of the Creator.

In creation there is an interconnectedness between life forms. The same structure and function of life exists in all of creation. The life-giving and life-sustaining veins of a leaf are to a tree as the life-giving and life-sustaining veins of a hand are to a person.

Nature has a simplicity, therefore, a great beauty.   –Richard Feynman

The structure and function of the veins in a leaf are similar to that of the veins in a hand. The leaf of a tree is connected to the hand of a person through the commonality of creation and through the commonality of the Creator. The web of the spider is a manifestation of nature's interconnectedness. The web is cast out in the fall as a means of harvesting sustenance for the impending scarcity of winter. The spider wraps its harvest in a bundle of web to be preserved until the needs of winter arrive. So too it is that we are created with the ability and the necessity

19. SPIDER WEB AND INSECTS

This is what I have asked of God for you: that you will be encouraged and knit together by strong ties of love,... COLOSSIANS 2:2 TLB

to harvest and preserve for the needs of winter. Like the spider's preparation for winter, the farmer harvests the alfalfa by collecting and gathering the hay into a bundle. The bundle of hay is then wrapped in a protective coating to preserve it for the winter needs of his livestock. Each life form on this planet has been created with the ability to sustain and preserve life.

Just as the earth undergoes the changes of season, so too it is that our lives undergo the changes of season. Our lives are sustained and preserved through the lush and bountiful glory of green and bloom to the colorful ending of growth and harvest to the silent, cold dormancy of winter. Each phase of life's season is a necessary component for all of creation to survive. Each form of life has been endowed by the Creator to adapt to, adjust to, and conform to the necessary changes in season in order to sustain its own life.

In all of nature there is a great diversity of life. In nature individual variation is the rule of creation. There is a reason and purpose behind the intricate order of all individuals of creation. Each variation contributing to and serving its own function and role in life. There is the ultimate raw and natural beauty and color of the wild flowers. There is the natural engineering and structural marvel of the insect world. There is the natural intricate, aerodynamic mechanisms of the winged birds. There is the complex chemistry and physiology for the extraction of oxygen from water which is mastered by the fishes. There is the phenomenal and intelligent, specialized development of the senses of sight, sound, and smell in the animal world. Each intricately specialized variation in nature is a kind unto itself. Each kind a necessary component in the order and chain of life and survival in nature.

The whole of life is equally dependent upon the specialization and unique individuality of each kind. There is in nature and life a reasoning, a rhyme, a rhythm, and a resonance for all kinds. Each individual kind dependent one upon the other to maintain the intricate balance of life itself. No one kind is less than or inferior in importance or magnitude to another kind in the preservation of the whole. There is an interdependency in all of nature and in all of life.

The intricate physical intelligence of nature in the world is also the same intricate physical intelligence within the physical body of man. The presence of these life-giving and life-sustaining forces were imparted to us as they were to all of natural life at creation. Modern science is only beginning to expose and unravel these mysteries of life. The magnitude of the capacity for the

20. MILKWEED POD: FIXED ORDER

Thus says the Lord, who gives the sun for light of day, the fixed order of the moon and the stars for light by night, who stirs up the sea so that its waves roar; the Lord of Hosts is His name!

JEREMIAH 31:35 NAS

body to heal itself from illness and injury is nearly incomprehensible.

I am convinced that when we immerse ourselves in and surround ourselves with the thoughts, the sites, the sounds, the smell, and the feel of our world, we become internally energized. Our resistance to disease, tolerance for pain, ability to reduce stress, capability to alleviate depression and in general experience a more complete life can in some ways be connected to our relationship with nature. The physiology of that relationship has been partially elucidated by modern medicine.

Our state of mind, level of awareness and perception, and state of consciousness, are responsible for the formation of our attitudes. Attitudes have a profound effect on our bodies, souls, and spirits. I think that we have the potential, through our attitudes about the order of life and the world, to more fully experience the greatness of life. Our attitudes are formed and developed as a result of our thoughts and beliefs, and from the sensory input from the world around us. Exposure of one's self to the sensory experience of nature helps evoke within our bodies, souls, and spirits many processes of healing and joy responsible for fulfillment and success.

The immune system becomes energized by producing more T-lymphocytes to fight cancer and infection. The brain produces increasing levels of endorphins, Dopamine, serotonin, and other neuro-transmitters which fight pain and alleviate depression. These chemical neuro-transmitters also stimulate the reward center in the brain which enables man to experience a sense of well-being, a sense of security, a sense of meaning, a sense of purpose and a general sense of competency. This reduction of stress reduces the levels of chemicals from the adrenal gland which when elevated can produce high blood pressure and heart disease.

But even more intriguing is the observation that when we see our own place in the order of our world, there follows a change in our own attitudes—a transformation from self-centeredness and egocentrism to that of equal consideration and respect for others and our surroundings. There follows a sense of smallness and humility. We see ourselves as not being separate from, but as an integral part, of the whole world. Therefore, a true relationship is established between us and creation.

In an attempt to further understand this tremendous potential for our fulfillment, let us consider the how and why of this relationship between us and creation. In order to demonstrate this principle, I would like to take you on a visual

21. Hay Stores

And if you will carefully obey all of His commandments that I am going to give you today, and if you will love the Lord your God with all your hearts and souls and will worship Him, then He will continue to send both the early and late rains that will produce wonderful crops of grain, grapes for your wine, and olive oil. He will give you lush pastureland for your cattle to graze, and you yourselves shall have plenty to eat and be fully content. DEUTERONOMY 11:13-15 TLB

tour of some of the simple sites I have found around me. These sites are an inspiration to me and I hope they will be to you also. When I thought God was gone and had forgotten me, these sites provided the evidence of His presence and provision to His creation—including my family and me.

There is a magnificent force behind all of life and creation. Creation has been shaped, molded, refined, preserved, and guided by that force. Life is able to sustain itself through the presence of that force. That force which allows life and mankind to exist in this ever-changing world is God. The only constant in this ever changing world and life is God. God provides for and sustains life in nature. God provides for and sustains the fish, the birds, the animals, and the plants on this planet. So it is that God sustains us through the many changes in our lives. So it is that God is the force behind creation, life, and survival. To see life is to see God. God reveals Himself to us through His creation of nature. To see nature is to see God.

For since the creation of the world, God's invisible qualities—his eternal power and divine nature—have been clearly seen, being understood from what has been made.

ROMANS 1:18 NIV

Therefore it is the exposure of our bodies, souls, and spirits to God in nature that helps form our attitudes—not the sensory experience of nature alone. It is God in nature who is responsible for the formation of our attitudes. It is no wonder then that our attitudes have such a profound effect on our lives. They are formed by our thoughts, beliefs, perceptions, consciousness, and awareness of God! How important is attitude to success in life?

ATTITUDE

The longer I live, the more I realize the impact of attitude on life. Attitude, to me, is more important than facts.

It is more important than the past, than education, than money, than circumstances, than failures, than successes, than what other people think or say or do. It is more important than appearance, giftedness, or skill. It will make or break a company... a church... a home... (or a hospital).

The remarkable thing is we have a choice every day regarding the attitude we will embrace for that day. We cannot change our past.... We cannot change the fact that people will act in a certain way. We cannot change the inevitable. The only thing we can

22. FALL

One day as the crowds were gathering, Jesus went up the hillside with His disciples and sat down and taught them there. "Will all your worries add a single moment to your life and why worry about your clothes? Look at the field lilies! They don't worry about theirs! Yet King Solomon in all his glory was not clothed as beautifully as they." MATTHEW 6:27-29 *TLB*

do is play on the one string we have, and that is our attitude....

I am convinced that life is 10% what happens to me, and 90% how I react to it. And so it is with you.... We are in charge of our Attitudes.

–Charles Swendoll

Just as the personal characteristics of a fine artisan or craftsman are revealed in his work, so too are the personal characteristics of God revealed in His work—nature. To be aware of nature as a manifestation of God is also to be aware of one's self as being a manifestation of God. The Mind and Intelligence that created the universe is that Mind which created you. That Mind is also present in every individual. For in the power and presence of that Mind exists the individual's unlimited and boundless potential. Just as theoretical physicists now view the universe as being infinite and unlimited, so too is the Mind behind the universe infinite and unlimited. Theoretical physicists view the Mind or Consciousness behind and present in the entire universe as omnipotent, omnipresent, and omniscient. That sounds like God to me! That Mind is God. God intends for that Mind of His to become activated and manifest in the life of every individual. Nature only tells us of the characteristics of that Mind and is only evidence of the presence of that Mind. God has a special plan by which He allows us to individually activate this inner infinite and immortal potential. God's plan for us is not only to reveal Himself to us through His creation, but also to relate to us in an intimate, personal way. The central question before mankind and us as individuals is: "How does He plan to accomplish this relationship?"

23. SQUIRREL
Jesus used this illustration:
"For everyone who asks, receives; and he who seeks, finds;"... LUKE 11:10 TLB

24. OTTO

And God said, "Let us make man in our image, after our likeness."
GENESIS 1:26 KJV

What is man, that Thou doest take thought of him? And the son of man, that Thou doest care for him? Yet Thou hast made him a little lower than the angels, and hast crowned him to have dominion over the works of Thy hands; Thou hast put all things under his feet...O Lord, our Lord, how excellent is Thy name in all the earth!
PSALM 8:4-9 KJV

4 • Creation of Spirit and Soul: Mankind's Relationship With the Creator

The Creator's supreme creation is mankind. When one considers the entire spectrum and diversity of life which is about us, its magnitude seems limitless. It is both awe-inspiring and extremely humbling to realize that among the vast things of life the Creator's unchanging purpose has been to catapult us to the top of life's ladder. For at our creation, we were created in God's own image.

We, like nature, are created with a physical body. Initially we were created containing the elements of all other life. Our physical bodies have in common with the physical world the elements of carbon, hydrogen, oxygen, and nitrogen. These are the elements common to all forms of life. We also were created with a soul which is made up of mind, will, and emotions. Unlike nature, but like God, we have also been imparted a spirit. Unlike all other kinds of creation at the creation of man, God breathed into mankind the presence of His own Spirit. Humans have within themselves a part of the very spirit of God. God Himself is Spirit. God did so to create a mechanism to fulfill His own need to love and be loved. Through the presence of His Spirit, God is able to love us and in turn has enabled us to love Him.

One of the functions of the Spirit is to impart to humans a sense of consciousness. Consciousness is the capacity to have, share, and experience the presence of love, joy, peace, patience, kindness, goodness, faithfulness, gentleness, and self control. These qualities are the inner thoughts and desires of our spirits. These qualities are perfect in God who is Spirit. The most important purpose of these is both to provide us with a spiritual way to give our love to God and to receive God's love; but also to provide God with a spiritual way to give His love to us and receive our love. It is in our spirit where the desire to know God resides. He has chosen humans over all other creatures to which He will reveal Himself and with whom He will develop a relationship. It is from our spirits that our desire to have a relationship with God emanates.

Just as there is an interconnectedness in all of nature, there too is an interconnectedness between our bodies, souls, and spirits. If there is an alteration in the body of man, there follows an equal alteration in our souls. If there is a change in our spirits, there follows a change in our bodies and souls. As Aristotle had observed long ago, the body and soul react sympathetically upon each other.

A change in the state of the soul produces a change in the shape of the body. And conversely a change in the shape of the body produces a change in the state of the soul.

—Aristotle

Our state of consciousness has a profound effect on the status of our bodies, souls, and spirits. Our state of consciousness is affected by the input from our senses and from our thoughts, desires and beliefs. The way we perceive the world about us is through the input of our senses. Our awareness of self and the world is partly formed by what we see, hear, smell, taste, and feel. Our state of consciousness is equally affected by the input of our spirits. It is from our spirits that our thoughts, desires and beliefs exert their effect on our bodies. This intricate relationship has long been recognized and a concern to both science and medicine.

For this is the great error of our day in the treatment of the human body, that physicians separate the soul from the body.

—Plato

Even today modern medicine is only beginning to fully understand, recognize, and appreciate the relationships between the body, soul, and spirit in its treatment of the ill and afflicted person. Optimal health, healing, and happiness exists when there is a balance, a rhythm, and a resonance between body, soul, and spirit.

Medical studies have shown that patients admitted to hospital rooms with windows required less pain medications, suffered fewer medical complications, and were discharged from the hospital earlier than those admitted to hospital rooms without windows. Patient's state of consciousness is affected by the input from their senses—by what they see, what they hear, what they smell, and also by what they taste and feel. In this circumstance we can see how patient's state of consciousness has affected the status of their bodies.

Medical research has only recently demonstrated that 40% to 50% of people who have heart attacks do not have the presence of risk factors such as high cholesterol, hypertension, diabetes, smoking, or family history for heart disease. Further studies have shown that the majority of heart attacks occur at 9:00 AM on Monday morning. People who experience these life-threatening heart attacks have been found to suffer from unhappiness, unfulfillment, and anxiety in their jobs. Therefore, the catastrophe of their heart attack is precipitated by their conscious confrontation with Monday morning stress, anxiety, unfulfillment and unhappiness.

People's state of consciousness has affected the status of their bodies.

Medical studies done in nurseries have shown that babies who are held, caressed, massaged, and talked to and generally loved, have a more rapid growth rate and fewer medical complications. Studies done in the past in orphanages and nurseries have shown that in some instances babies whose care did not include physical love and personal affection had a higher incidence of sickness, and many actually died.

Many children who have experienced chronic illnesses and prolonged separation from their loved ones have developed a disorder called Deprivation Dwarfism. These children despite meticulous medical care and exact nutritional supplementation, lost weight, and had delayed mental, social, and physical growth and development. When given love and affection, the effects of this disorder were reversed and corrected. So, the shape of the body of man is connected to the state of his conscious perception of love.

Numerous scientific and medical studies also document that the conscious presence of faith, hope, and love have a profound effect on the body. The presence of faith and hope have been found to reduce the ill-effects of stress, energize the immune system to better fight cancer and

25. Elwin and Hazel

Then the Lord God said, "It is not good for the man to be alone; I will make him a helper suitable for him." And the Lord God fashioned into a woman the rib which he had taken from the man, and brought her to him. And the man said, "This is now bone of my bones, and flesh of my flesh; She shall be called woman because she was taken out of man." For this cause a man shall leave his father and mother and shall cleave to his wife; and they shall become one flesh.
Genesis 2:18,22-24 NAS

infection, and combat depression and give-up-itis. In fact, the largest study of its kind has recently shown that three of the factors common to people who live the longest are faith, hope, and love. In that study of people over 100 years of age, they had in common a personal belief system which was based on faith and hope, and sustained loving relationships in their lives. Other studies show that there is a decreased incidence of heart disease in men with a loving marital relationship. Men whose marriages are characterized by strife, discord, anger, and hostility have a higher incidence of heart attacks. At the same time, women survive breast cancer at a higher rate when surrounded by loving, caring relationships.

It has long been recognized that the effective and meaningful dispensation of hope to the sick and afflicted has the capacity to evoke the processes of healing and recovery. Dr. William S. Middleton, emeritus dean of the University of Wisconsin Medical School, and both my father's and my personal mentor, emphasized the importance of hope in the treatment of patients when he stated:

> He is the best physician who is the best inspirer of hope.   –William S. Middleton, M.D.

I have observed on many occasions that the removal of hope is equivalent to the removal of life itself. The presence of hope is a necessary component of life.

Now, God created us with specific physical needs and placed us in an environment rich and abundant in these elements of our needs. We require oxygen to survive. The atmosphere about our planet has an abundance of oxygen. We require water to survive. The physical environment on earth has an abundance of water. The same simple reasoning can be used for all of our physical needs and the provision of these needs by the Creator.

But remember, when we were created, we were created in the image of the Creator Himself—God. God is Spirit. Spirit is consciousness. We have a consciousness which not only has a profound affect on our physical bodies but has needs of its own. Just as the physical body has a fundamental need for oxygen, so too do our spirits have a fundamental need for love. As the evidence just presented indicates, the presence of love can be a significant factor in determining health, and in fact can be a determining factor in life or death. Many medical experts conclude that our greatest need is to love and be loved. God Himself has these individual needs. No wonder that His master plan and Will for us would be to devise a way for a loving relationship to develop between us and Him.

26. PROTECTION

This I declare, that He alone is my refuge, my place of safety; He is my God, and I am trusting Him.... He will shield you with His wings! They will shelter you. His faithful promises are your armor. PSALM 91:4 TLB

Thy Word is a lamp unto my feet, and a light unto my path. PSALM 119:104 NIV

5 ◆ God's Word

God reveals Himself to us through His Word. The Bible is the Will of God for us. The Bible is the Word of God.

In the beginning was the Word and the Word was with God and the Word was God. JOHN 1:1 NIV

Just as the character of God is revealed through His workmanship of creation, so is His character revealed through His Word. As individuals, we reveal our person by what we say. God reveals His Person to us through His Word. His Word is our factual account of what He says. His Word is then a factual account of what He is. But most importantly, His Word is a factual account of who He is.

God's Word not only discloses what He says to mankind in general, but also what He says specifically to each of us as individuals. God's Word is His personal form of communication with us. God talks to us as individuals through His Word. God's Word is His talk and is His voice to each of us as His creation.

27. Owl

And I, if I be lifted up from the earth,
will draw all men unto Me.
JOHN 12:32 KJV

The Bible is the Will of God for our lives. It contains our inheritance. Just as we would need to read our own dad's will, in order to learn of our inheritance, we also need to read God's Will—the Will of our Heavenly Father is for us to learn of our inheritance from Him. Is it possible that a person is rich from an inheritance without even knowing it? Yes!! If that person fails to read and learn the contents of the will. God's Will for you and me is revealed in His Word. It tells us what every person looks for.

> *The whole Bible was given to us by inspiration from God and is useful to teach us what is true and to make us realize what is wrong in our lives; it straightens us out and helps us do what is right. It is God's way of making us well prepared at every point, fully equipped to do good to everyone.* II TIMOTHY 3:16-17 TLB

I have found this to be the hidden desire of every human kind, especially myself—to do good and to do what is right in life.

Medicine has long recognized the importance of God's Word in the Bible. Sir William Osler, the father of modern medicine, challenged students of medicine to master three works in order to serve the needs of mankind: master the textbook of medicine to provide knowledge and understanding of the body of man, master the works of Shakespeare to gain knowledge and understanding of the nature of mankind, and master the Bible to gain knowledge and understanding of the spirit of mankind and God. One of Dr. Middleton's advised preoccupations for the physician was to become engaged in Biblical study. From Plato to Aristotle to Hippocrates to Sir William Osler to Dr. Middleton to today, medicine has known of mankind's spirit, its relationship to the body and soul, and the necessity to administer to its needs.

The factual basis of knowledge regarding the interplay between the spirit, soul, body and the whole of life is God's Word. God's spoken Word is life. Just as He spoke creation into being, His spoken Word created life.

The Bible was written over a 1600 year span, over sixty generations, by forty authors from every walk of life including kings, peasants, philosophers, fishermen, poets, statesmen, scholars, and a physician, in times of war and peace, during different moods from joy to sorrow, on three continents, Asia, Africa and Europe, and in three languages.

The survival of the Word of God against all powers and forces of opposition is evidence for its Divine Origin.

Infidels for 1800 years have been refuting and overthrowing this Book, and yet it stands today as solid as a rock. Its circulation increases, and it is more loved and cherished and read today than ever before. Infidels, with all their assaults, make about as much impression on this Book as a man with a tack hammer would on the Pyramids of Egypt. When the French monarch proposed the persecution of the Christians in his domain, an old statesman and warrior said to him, "Sire, the Church of God is an anvil that has worn out many hammers." So the hammers of infidels have been pecking away at this Book for ages, but the hammers are worn out, and the anvil still endures. If this Book had not been the Book of God, men would have destroyed it long ago. Emperors and poets, kings and priests, princes and rulers, have all tried their hand at it; they die and the Book still lives.

–H.L. Hastings, cited by John W. Lea

The Bible is entirely unique in its prophecy: the foretelling of circumstances, events, persons, and happenings to the human race.

Whatever one may think of the authority of and the message printed in this book we call the Bible, there is world-wide agreement that in more ways than one it is the most remarkable volume that has ever been produced in these some 5,000 years of writing on the part of the human race.

It is the only volume ever produced by man or a group of men in which it is to be found a large body of prophecies relating to individual nations, to Israel, to all the peoples of the earth, to certain cities, and to the coming of One who was to be the Messiah. The ancient world had many different devices for determining the future known as divinations, but not in the entire gamut of Greek and Latin literature, even though they used the words prophet and prophecy, can we find any real specific prophecy of a great historic event to come in the distant future, nor any prophecy of a Savior to arise in the human race....

Mohammedism cannot point to any prophecies of the coming of Mohammed uttered hundreds of years before his birth. Neither can the founders of any cult in this country rightly identify any ancient text specifically foretelling their appearance.

–Wilbur Smith, *The Incomparable Book,* Beacon Publications

It's subject matter includes hundreds of controversial subjects. A controversial subject is one which would create opposing beliefs, thoughts, and opinions when mentioned or discussed. Biblical authors spoke on hundreds of controversial subjects with harmony and continuity from Genesis to Revelation. There is one unfolding story: God's redemption of man through Christ.

The most reassuring fact of Biblical direction as it affects those of us who listen to it as a guide for our lives is its solidarity and stability.

Heaven and earth shall pass away, but My words shall never pass away.
Matthew 24:35 nas

Most simplistically and profoundly the Word of God is a revelation to us of God's everlasting absolute truth.

The sum of Thy Word is truth and every one of Thy righteous ordinances is everlasting.
Psalm 119:160 nas

God also reveals Himself to us in a much more personal and intimate way. Even more intimate than through His creation and through His very Word. God's ultimate revelation to us is through a personal relationship. Why relate to us through a relationship?

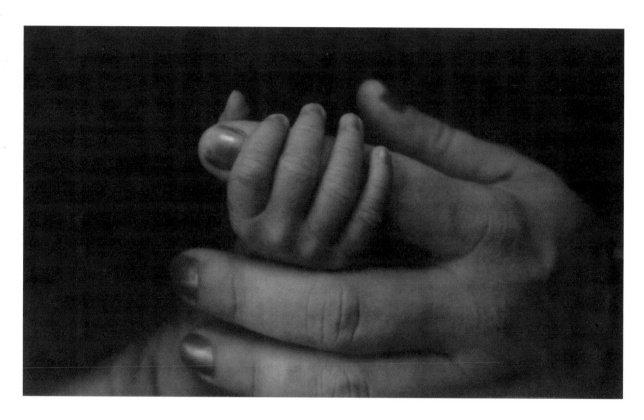

28. MOTHER AND CHILD

For Thou didst form my inward parts; Thou didst weave me in my mother's womb. I will give thanks to Thee, for I am fearfully and wonderfully made; How precious also are Thy thoughts to me, O God.
PSALM 139:13,14,17 KJV

6 • The Foundation of Relationships

The Creator created us with natural biological, social, psychological and spiritual inclinations to seek out individual relationships. We were created with the natural biological, social, psychological, and spiritual tendencies to pattern ourselves and our relationships with individuals. It is from our souls and spirits that these needs, necessities, and tendencies originate. It is only natural then, that as a result of creation, we would be born into relationships. Hence, the necessity for the human family. The human family to a great extent serves as the earliest formation place for an individual's emotional and personality development.

> The family forms the earliest and most persistent influence that encompasses the still unformed infant and small child for whom the parents' ways and the family ways are the way of life, the only way he knows. All subsequent experiences are perceived, understood and reacted to emotionally according to the foundations established in the family. The family ways and the child's patterns of reacting to them become so integrally incorporated in the child that they can be

29. GEESE

His unchanging plan has always been to adopt us into His own family by sending Jesus Christ to die for us. And He did this because He wanted to! EPHESIANS 1:5 TLV

considered determinants of his constitutional make-up difficult to differentiate from the genetic biological influences with which they interrelate.

–The Person by Theodore Litz, Professor and Chairman, Department of Psychiatry, Yale University School of Medicine

The family's influence on the individual is profound. However, the Creator through the development of our complex and intricate psychosocial mind reserves the right to provide a means for modification and change. The structure and function of human families is as diverse as that for the make-up of individuals. One absolute, which I have observed for both families and individuals, is that neither exists in a perfect form. If individuals were constrained and limited in their pursuit of the mastery of survival by unchangeable, irreparable qualities imparted to them only by their families, humans as individuals, and mankind in general would be doomed. This would be an exceedingly unfair system since individuals cannot pick their families. This system would also lead to a dead-end for all of mankind since an individual would be incapable of rising above the circumstance from which he came. Unfortunately, these are the very psycho-logical, social, intellectual, and physical constraints imposed upon life in the world.

In God's infinite wisdom, he has provided an escape and an exclusion from these constraints. This does not mean, however, that God intends for us to annihilate, reject or dispose of all of those characteristics imparted to us by our families. The value of a person, and the wealth of an individual, are in large measure imparted by the endowment from family, which is made up of both genetic and those factors of nurture which make up the person. This endowment is not totally set in stone at birth. It can be changed throughout life. The brain remains pliable. This process of change is known as experiential brain development. Studies have shown that the anatomy and physiology of an individual's brain can be changed by the way he chooses to think, feel, and act. The actual structure and function of the brain can be changed and modified by an individual's experience. For those characteristics which are detrimental to the individual's accomplishing and enjoying the fullness of life, God has allowed us a mechanism by which to reshape, re-mold and remodel those characteristics from our family endowment which will enable us to soar to greater heights.

30. Three Young Boys   31. Three Old Men

Therefore, if any man be in Christ, he is a new creature: Old things are passed away behold, all things are become new. II Corinthians 5:17 KJV

He has a more perfect plan for us.

Just as He has revealed His Presence to all of mankind through the magnitude of His creation, and through the profound truth and wisdom of His Word, He has also insured that every individual would seek out a personal knowledge of Him. He has insured this by creating within mankind the necessity for love. But what is love? Where is love? How does mankind obtain love?

And so we know and rely on the love God has for us. God is love! Whoever lives in love lives in God and God in him. I John 4:16 NIV

Yes, this is a Biblical definition of love—God is love! Therefore, love is that which holds all together. Love is that force responsible for all actions and interactions in the universe and in the life of individuals. Knowledgeable scientists are in agreement with this all important central message of the Bible.

If one looks deep enough, the thread of truth and love arising from God is woven into the fabric of all human pursuits.

The need, necessity, and the personal inclinations for us to seek loving interpersonal relationships sets the stage for God's ultimate revelation to us. God develops a plan to relate to us in a manner in which we were created and predestined to need and to seek out. We were created with the need and the necessity to relate to God as a person. Does God reveal Himself to us as a person? Does He reveal Himself to us as a person of love? How does God reveal Himself to us as a person of love? How does He relate to us in a way through which we can exercise our natural born tendencies to relate interpersonally?

32. SUNBURST WITH SILVER LINING

But without faith it is impossible to please Him; for he that cometh to God must believe that He is [the Creator] and that He is a rewarder of them that diligently seek Him. HEBREWS 11:6 KJV

7 ◆ God's Intimacy With Mankind: Faith, Hope, and Love

But God intends to be more intimate and personal with His supreme creation of humankind. God's unchanging plan and reason for the creation of mankind has been to establish a being with which He could develop a spiritual, loving interpersonal relationship. His plan from the beginning has been to provide His love to us with the desire for us to relate back to Him through love. He created us with the predisposition to relate to our own kind. Therefore, He came to us in the form of our own kind. God came to us as a Person in the form of His Son, Jesus.

And Christ became a human being and lived here on Earth among us and was full of loving forgiveness and truth. And some of us have seen his glory—the glory of the only son of the Heavenly Father. JOHN 1:14 TLB

For in Christ there is all of God in a human body, so you have everything when you have Christ and you are filled with God through your union with Christ. COLOSSIANS 1:9-10 TLB

Christ is the exact likeness of the unseen God. COLOSSIANS 1:15 TLB

33. Baby Birds

O sing to the Lord a new song,…The Lord has made known His salvation, … then shout joyfully to the Lord, all the earth; Break forth and sing for joy and sing praises. Psalm 98:1,2,4 NAS

It is through the life of Jesus that we see how to love. His life is our living demonstration of love in action. God intends for us to have our own interpersonal relationships, not based on our natural emotions such as resentment, envy, jealousy, hate or hostility; but in the way Jesus, through his own interpersonal relationships, taught us, and through His life demonstrated to us, how to relate one to another.

Below are the characteristics of Godly love and in fact the characteristics exemplified in the historical accounts of the life and relationships of Jesus.

Love is very patient and kind. Never jealous or envious, never boastful or proud, never haughty, or selfish, or rude. Love does not demand its own way. It is not irritable or touchy. It does not hold grudges and will hardly even notice when others do it wrong. It is never glad about injustice but rejoices whenever truth wins out. If you love someone, you will be loyal to him no matter what the cost. You will always believe in him, always expect the best of him, and always stand your ground in defending him.
I Corinthians 13:4-7 TLB

These are the very personal characteristics which our Creator intends for us to incorporate into our emotional and personality development. God has given us these images of His love so that we might implement them as a basis for our own interpersonal relationships. The force, power and transforming impact that these characteristics have on the individual human is beyond measure. These characteristics represent the strongest force affecting our lives.

I have the ultimate privilege of caring for the lives of people through the practice of medicine. My duty is to participate in the entire spectrum of human life. My privilege is to attend people from conception through life to death. I have observed and experienced that the lives of people are sustained through illness, injury, trials and tragedy by the operation of love. I have observed and experienced that a life of success, accomplishment, position, stature and health without love is never a truly fulfilling life. Faith and hope augment the life-sustaining effects of love. People's response to illness and disease can significantly be energized through the operation of faith, hope, and love. At all times in life we need God. But especially in the face of physical and emotional sufferings, faith, hope, and love may be our most potent medicine.

There exists physiological and experimental evidence to suggest that the dispensation of faith, hope, and love acts as a potent medicine. In man's mid-brain, there exists, in addition to the reward center (previously mentioned), the center responsible for self-preservation and the center in control of the human will. Stimulation of these centers results in a strong drive to survive. A lack of stimulation or a suppression of these centers results in a loss of the drive to survive and a loss of the will to live.

Why does a sick and afflicted person fight, dig, scratch and grasp for life? Because that person has a strong stimulation of his or her self-preservation center and the center for the will. These centers are stimulated by faith, hope, and love. These centers are turned off by the negative biochemical effects produced by guilt, resentment, anger, jealousy, isolation, fear, and rejection. These relationships have been extensively studied in prisoners of war. Prisoners of war subjected to long periods of isolation and these negative psychological tactics lose the will to live and lose their innate drive to preserve themselves. They have been described as apathetic, hollow, empty and as though they were walking corpses. This syndrome has been described as "give-up-itis" and appears shortly before actual death.

For another clinical example of the effects a deprivation of love, faith, and hope have on the

human, let's consider Deprivation Dwarfism. This is a syndrome described in chronically ill children after prolonged hospitalization. These children have been deprived of their usual amount of emotional, psychological and physical reinforcement from their loved ones. As a result of their prolonged hospital treatment, they have become isolated. Isolation and deprivation of love leads to loneliness. Loneliness leads to a loss of faith. Loss of faith leads to a lack of hope. Deprivation of love, faith and hope results in a retardation of physical, emotional, and intellectual growth and development. In spite of meticulous medical care and balanced nutritional support, these children still developed this syndrome of retarded emotional, mental and physical growth and development.

Some children who have manifested this syndrome have died. Others, when treated with greater engagement, greater involvement, greater support, and greater reinforcement of love from their families and hospital staff, have not only arrested the effects of this syndrome, but have effectively reversed its effects. One can only conclude that such a condition is the result of markedly altered and abnormal human physiology induced by the deprivation of love, faith, and hope. Humans need love, faith, and hope. God has provided the mechanism by which we can obtain these necessities of life.

I have observed this same syndrome in many chronically ill, chronically depressed, and severely stressed patients. These patients without exception lack a human support system which is involved, engaged, and loving. They also, without exception, lack a personal belief system which is based on and encourages the action of faith, hope, and love. When there is a will there seems to be a way.

Conversely, it seems that when there is no will there is no perceived way. Eliminate the biochemical effects of these factors on the human brain, and the battle for life can easily and sometimes willfully be given up. But replace isolation, fear, guilt, resentment, anger, jealousy and rejection with involvement, engagement, security, loyalty, and acceptance, and the balance can be tilted towards survival and life. The latter factors produce biochemical effects in the brain which stimulate the center for self-preservation and strengthen the action of the human will. These centers in turn help activate, stimulate, and regulate many other functions in the body such as the brain itself, the heart, the lungs, the kidney, and the immune response which are all necessary to sustain life in the face of disease, illness, and injury.

Yes, our ability to experience the fullness of faith, hope, and love can be a determining factor between recovery versus disability and life versus death.

I have observed this repeatedly at the patient's bedside. The patient is the victim of an accident or injury. On the one hand the patient is supported by a loving, caring, hopeful, positive healthcare team. His employer reinforces his job security and validates his personal importance. His family is supportive and encouraging, and motivates his recovery. The patient goes on to full rehabilitation and recovery. Dr. Middleton documented his observation and appreciation of these dynamics in his following quote:

> The objective criteria, now under consideration by the several agencies engaged in its study, are incapable of measuring the imponderable values of human sympathy and compassion. The output of the understanding heart of the true physician and the good nurse cannot be measured or approximated by any available method. Nonetheless, this intangible force may be a vital, yes, a determining factor in life and death.
>
> –William S. Middleton, M.D.

On the other hand, perhaps the patient per-

34. GROUNDHOGS

Thy loving kindness and Thy Truth will continually preserve me. PSALM 40:11 *KJV*

ceives that he is victimized, unappreciated and his position of employment jeopardized by his employer. He feels rejected and separated by an uninvolved, disinterested family. The patient perceives himself as being under-served and inappropriately cared for by his team of health-care providers. This patient does not respond to rehabilitation, defies recovery, and goes on to disability.

A critical illness has stricken a person. All that medicine has to offer has been implemented. The outcome hangs in the balance. One patient is surrounded by caring, affectionate care-givers who offer expressions and affections of hope, faith, and love. A supportive, involved, and loving family holds a bedside vigil. The balance is tipped towards life. A similarly ill person is supported by all of the same science but in a sterile, uninvolved and dis-attached environment. The balance is tipped towards demise. Numerous recent scientific studies indicate that cancer victims have a higher cure rate, longer survival, and less painful course of their illness when surrounded by faith, hope and love.

God's revelation of love through His Son is intended to be our example to follow. When Jesus is incorporated into a human life, God's love lives through that life. Humans are born with the necessity to satisfy their thirst for love. Jesus is the river of flowing waters from which we are predestined to drink in order to satisfy our thirst. Once we have taken in the waters of His love and life, our lives can become a reservoir and wellspring of God's love. The effects of that water produce the fruits of faith, hope, and love. Faith, hope, and love are capable of sustaining health and life itself. Not only for our individual selves, but also for those who become the recipients of that faith, hope, and love. We are to freely share these life-determining fruits to those around us, who are in need and who are in distress. For some, the personal manifestation of faith, hope, and love seen in the lives of others may be their only glimpse of the living God.

Christmas

35. CROSS

Jesus answered and said, "For God so loved the world that He gave His only begotten Son, that whosoever believeth in Him should not perish, but have everlasting life." JOHN 3:16 KJV

8 ◆ The Christmas Gift of Love and Life

The true gift of Christmas is to see God's love for us through the life, death, and resurrection of His Son, Jesus. Even more simplistically, it is essential that we as individuals see this happening as an historical event and not merely as some spiritual aberration. History proves that these events actually happened. Take note of these historically based thoughts about Jesus.

> Some writers may toy with the fancy of a "Christ myth," but they do not do so on the ground of historical evidence. The historicity of Christ is as axiomatic for an unbiased historian as the historicity of Julius Caesar. It is not historians who propagate the "Christ myth" theories.
>
> –F.F. Bruce

A Roman historian, Cornelius Tacitus, in 112 A.D. recorded these observations.

> Hence to suppress the rumor, he falsely charged with guilt, and punished with the most exquisite torture, the persons commonly called

36. SUNFLOWER

A merry heart doeth good like a medicine… PROVERBS 17:22 KJV

Christians, who were hated for their enormities. Christus, the founder of the name, was put to death by Pontius Pilate, procurator of Judea in the reign of Tiberius.

The most notable Jewish historian, Flavius Josephus, recorded the following:

Now there was about this time Jesus, a wise man, if it be lawful to call him a man, for he was a doer of wonderful works, a teacher of such men as received the truth with pleasure. He drew over to him both many of the Jews and many of the Gentiles. He was the Christ, and when Pilate, at the suggestion of the principal men among us, had condemned him to the cross, those that loved him at the first, did not forsake him; for he appeared to them alive again the third day; as the divine prophets had foretold these and ten thousand other wonderful things concerning him. And the tribe of Christian so named for him, are not extinct at this day.

–*Antiquities XVIII,* early second century

The Person of these monumental events has had a more profound influence on human society than any other person historically studied over the last 2,000 years.

This Jesus of Nazareth, without money and arms, conquered more millions than Alexander, Caesar, Mohammed, and Napoleon; without science and learning, He shed more light on things human and divine than all philosophers and scholars combined; without the eloquence of schools, He spoke such words of life as were never spoken before or since, and produced effects which lie beyond the reach of orator or poet; without writing a single line, He set more pens in motion, and furnished themes for more sermons, orations, discussions, learned volumes, works of art, and songs of praise, than the whole army of great men of ancient and modern times.

–Philip Schaff in *The Person of Christ,* American Tract Society, 1913.

But more importantly, this Person and these events occurred for individual persons—these events occurred for you and me.

Dear Friends, Let us love one another, for love comes from God. Every one who loves has been born of God and knows God. Whoever does not love does not know God because God is love. This is how God showed His love among us. He sent His one and only Son into the world that

37. A CARING SHEPHERD

Dear Children, Let us not love with words or tongue but with action and in truth. I JOHN 3:18 NIV

we might live through Him. This is love: not that we loved God but that He loved us and sent His Son as an atoning sacrifice for our sins.
I JOHN 4:7-10 NIV

The fulfillment of that gift is the present day revelation of that love from one person to another. Just as the force of God's hand has shaped and molded all of life's forms on Earth, God's love shaped and expressed between peoples has the potential to transform human life on Earth. God's order is for us to recognize His love for us so that we in turn can love Him. This in turn allows us the capacity to love each other. God is a God of action! He calls us to action in implementing His plan for our relationships.

Dear Children, Let us not love with words or tongue but with action and in truth.
I JOHN 3:18 NIV

Of all of the maladies and afflictions and sufferings of human life, the most devastating and painful originate from disordered and chaotic human relationships. God's plan is for us to relate to one another from the basis of love for one another.

Dear Friends, Since God so loved us, we also ought to love one another. No one has ever seen God, but if we love one another God lives in us and His love is made complete in us.
I JOHN 4:11 NIV

We love because He first loved us. If someone says I love God yet hates his brother he is a liar. For anyone who does not love his brother whom he has seen cannot love God whom he has not seen. And He has given us this command. Whoever loves God must also love his brother. I JOHN 4:19-21 NIV

The first part of the Christmas gift is the life of Jesus. The life of Jesus is our living demonstration of love in action. This living gift of love is for you and me. God's plan is for Jesus to live through us. It is through our relationship with Jesus that we as individual humans become capable of giving life to love. God's plan and Will for our lives is to enable us to manifest this gift by loving each other. This action is the evidence for our relationship with God through the life of Jesus. Love's action in life is also the evidence for the fact that Jesus is alive today. When we love each other, it shows that the Person and power of Jesus is here and is alive and well today.

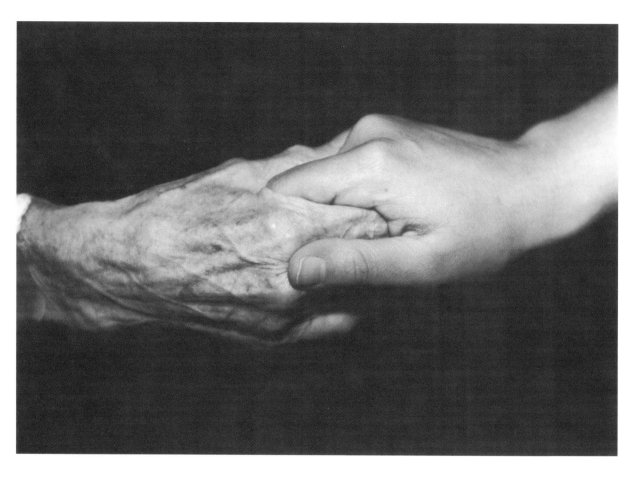

38. HOLDING HANDS

Jesus instructed them, saying, "Freely ye have received, freely give." MATTHEW 10:5,8 KJV

9 ♦ The Christmas Gift of Love and Forgiveness

For the second part of the gift, it is through the death of Jesus that God has shown an unimaginable degree of love. The thought of intentionally and consciously offering the life of one's own child for a cause to benefit others is an extremely painful one, one I personally found impossible to comprehend. It is a true measure of the love that God has for us as humans, but He allowed this human sacrifice of His Son for individuals like you and me.

Jesus' death on the cross is the ultimate expression of God's loving hand from the center of the universe touching earth and in fact touching individuals. It took Jesus' death on the cross to transform and perfect our spirits. All of us as individuals at some time in our lives confront our sinful nature. Our conscience reveals to us—we are sinners. When we recognize our own sinful nature, in time, we seek a resolution for our sins.

You see, just after man was created, he chose to disobey God. Man being made in the image of God was created perfectly. There was in Adam perfect harmony between his perfect body, his perfect soul, and his perfect spirit which led to a state of perfect health. When Adam chose to disobey God, sin entered the world and perfection came to an end.

When Adam sinned, sin entered the entire human race. His sin spread death throughout all the world so everything began to grow old and die, for all have sinned. ROMANS 5:12 TLB

All disease, illness, affliction, and death is a manifestation of Adam's original sin. From that time forward, we became separated from God. All of life, and in fact all of nature, were originally created in perfection. What was natural was perfection. So all imperfections in life and nature today are actually unnatural occurrences. Death, disease, destruction, pain, and suffering are not natural occurrences by God's design. Bigotry, prejudice, and hate are not natural occurrences by God's design. Wars with mass destruction against humankind are not natural occurrences by God's design. God did not create life intending for life to destroy itself. God's natural plan for us and for nature was perfect and perpetual health and life. Life's destruction in suffering, disease, and death resulted from the exercise of Adam's own free will. The unnatural degradation of nature, health and life is a consequence of humankind's choice through free will to disobey

the authority of God. Our physical bodies lost their perfection and became susceptible to the unnatural biological forces of illness, disease, affliction and death. After Adam's sin of disobedience to God, cancer, diabetes, heart disease, emphysema, strokes, high blood pressure, pneumonia, depression and all other physical and mental diseases entered the human race. Likewise, when Adam disobeyed God His perfect spirit in us became imperfect and incomplete.

Now, this death was obviously not an instant physical death because the seed of Adam and Eve went on to populate the earth. But from that day of disobedience to God, Adam and all of us became destined to live a physical life only to die a physical death. As we see today, physical disease, destruction, and death is the universal experience of humankind. But, the central point to be made is that this universal experience of physical death is not the natural plan of God. Nor is it God's final plan for our physical bodies. Similarly from that day of disobedience to God, Adam and mankind became likewise spiritually dead. But neither is spiritual death God's final plan for our spirits. But, our spirits became weak and incapable of following the perfect Will of God. Our spirit with all of its power and force became capable of being perverted and used for works and deeds against God Himself. We became afflicted with spiritual illnesses as we did with physical illnesses. Our spirit became susceptible to and open to the following of false gods. Our human spirit, and in fact our basic human nature, became bent on serving self and the anti-god of this world, Satan. But remember, Satan takes on many disguises and often appears to be like God. That is how he deceived Eve in the Garden of Eden which led to the fall of Adam and spiritual death of mankind in the first place. Our state of spiritual weakness also rendered our spiritual powers to be used and implemented for reasons and purposes other than to accomplish the perfect Will of God. Our spirit became naturally inclined to be used by Satan.

But when you follow your own wrong inclinations, your lives will produce these evil results: impure thoughts, eagerness for lustful pleasure, idolatry, spiritism (that is, encouraging the activity of demons), hatred and fighting, jealousy and anger, constant effort to get the best for yourself, complaints and criticisms, the feeling that everyone else is wrong except those in your own little group—and there will be wrong doctrine, envy, murder, drunkenness, wild parties, and all that sort of thing. Let me tell you again as I have before, that anyone living that

sort of life will not inherit the kingdom of God.
GALATIANS 5:19-21 TLB

But in His love for us, God devised a plan to bridge the gap between the imperfect, incomplete spirit, or human spirit, and God's own perfect Spirit—Holy Spirit..

I advise you to obey the Holy Spirit's instructions. He will tell you where to go and what to do, and then you won't always be doing the wrong things your evil nature wants you to. For we naturally love to do evil things that are just the opposite from the things that the Holy Spirit tells us to do; and the good things we want to do when the Spirit has His way with us are just the opposite of our natural desires. These two forces within us are constantly fighting each other to win control of us, and our wishes are never free from their pressures. When you are guided by the Holy Spirit, you need no longer force yourself to obey Jewish laws....

But when the Holy Spirit controls our lives he will produce this kind of fruit in us: love, joy, peace, patience, kindness, goodness, faithfulness, gentleness and self-control; and here there is no conflict with Jewish laws.
GALATIANS 5:16-18, 22-23 TLB

39. THE SERPENT AND THE FRUIT

Now the serpent was more subtle than any beast of the field which the Lord God had made... GEN. 3:1 NAS

Let no one say when he is tempted, "I am being tempted by God;" for God cannot be tempted by evil, and He Himself does not tempt anyone. But each one is tempted when he is carried away and enticed by his own lust. Then when lust has conceived, it gives birth to sin; and when sin is accomplished, it brings forth death. JAMES 1:13-15 NAS

But when the Holy Spirit controls our lives he will produce this kind of fruit in us: love, joy, peace, patience, kindness, goodness, faithfulness, gentleness and self-control;... GALATIANS 5:22 TLB

God's plan is to provide us with a way to restore our spirit to perfection. He does not intend for our spirits to be condemned to death in this world; but to be reunited, reinstated, and redeemed, with His own perfect Spirit through His Son, Christ. It is a matter of our own choice.

What a contrast between Adam and Christ who was yet to come! And what a difference between man's sin and God's forgiveness! For this one man, Adam brought death to many through his sin. But this one man, Jesus Christ, brought forgiveness to man through God's mercy. Adam's one sin brought the penalty of death to many, while Christ freely takes away many sins and gives glorious life instead. The sin of this one man, Adam, caused death to be king over all, but all who will take God's gift of forgiveness and acquittal are kings of life because of this one man, Jesus Christ. Yes, Adam's sin brought punishment to all, but Christ's righteousness makes men right with God, so that they can live. Adam caused many to be sinners because he disobeyed God and Christ caused many to be made acceptable to God because he obeyed.
ROMANS 5:15-19 TLB

That gap is bridged by the event of the crucifixion of Christ on the cross. By God's biblical law, forgiveness of sins follows a spotless, perfect, blood sacrifice of goats and calves.

And according to the Law, one may almost say, all things are cleansed with blood, and without shedding of blood, there is no forgiveness.
HEBREWS 9:22 NAS

This plan only foreshadowed God's ultimate perfect plan for us which called for the blood sacrifice of His own perfect Son.

But God showed His great love for us by sending Christ to die for us while we were still sinners and since by His blood he did all this for us as sinners, how much more will he do for us now that he has declared us not guilty? Now he will save us from all of God's wrath to come. And since, when we were his enemies, we were brought back to God by the death of his son, what blessings he must have for us now that we are his friends and He is living within us!
ROMANS 5:8-10 TLB

God allowed his Son, Jesus, to die as a sacrifice and payment for the sins of mankind and for the sins of individual persons. You see, all people are born into sin by their very creation as humankind. Adam passed his disobedience on to mankind—on to all of us. In His love for us, God

40. PRAIRIE DOGS

Bear ye one another's burdens, and so fulfill the law of Christ. GALATIANS 6:2 KJV

devised a plan, a method, and a mechanism by which we could achieve and accomplish forgiveness for our sins. A way in which we could reunite ourselves with God—to re-establish harmony between our own spirits and the Spirit of God.

It was through what His Son did that God cleared a path for everything to come to Him— all things in heaven and on earth—for Christ's death on the cross has made peace with God for all by His blood. This includes you who were once so far away from God. You were His enemies and hated Him and were separated from Him by your evil thoughts and actions, yet now, He has brought you back as His friends. He has done this through the death on the cross of his own human body and now as a result Christ has brought you into the very presence of God and you are standing there before Him with nothing left against you—nothing left that He could even chide you for, the only condition is that you fully believe the truth standing in it steadfast and firm, strong in the Lord, convinced of the good news that Jesus died for you and never shifting from trusting Him to save you. This is the wonderful news that came to each of you and is now spreading all over the world and I, Paul, have the joy of telling it to others. COLOSSIANS 1:20-23 TLB

So, it is by design revealed as God's plan in His Word that our only method and mechanism to get right with God is accomplished at the Cross of Christ. The Cross is the mechanism by which we humans are capable of resolving our own sins. God's incredible forgiveness is offered to you and me at the foot of that Cross.

The death of Christ as revealed in God's Word stands as a factual event. An event carried out before the eyes of mankind and individual persons, to be recorded as a fulfillment of God's plan to reinstate you and me in God's eyes. Simply by believing, this event accomplishes our correctness, our redemption, and our acceptance by God. God does not want us to miss this event and its redemptive meaning to our lives. It is by the death of His Son by which He came to forgive us. If you gave your child as a sacrifice for the life and fulfillment of all humans, would you not also demand a recognition of your child's sacrifice in death?

Life's fulfillment is impossible without forgiveness and a resolution of our personal sins. With guilt as a result of unforgiveness comes hate, death, and bondage. With forgiveness comes love, life, and freedom.

41. WATERFALL II

Jesus said, "Come unto Me, all ye that labor, and are heavy laden, and I will give you rest....For my yoke is easy and my burden is light." MATTHEW 11:28, 30 KJV

10 • Unresolved Guilt and Forgiveness

One of the most devastating and destructive human emotions is that of unresolved guilt. Unresolved guilt causes internal pain, self-condemnation, shame, paranoia, despondency, and eventually a smothering of the flame of life. Unresolved guilt is capable of inducing certain forms of mental illness including neuroses, depression, and full-blown psychosis and suicide. I have observed human life's vigor, involvement, engagement, contribution and productivity extinguished by the presence of unresolved guilt.

The scientific, medical, and physiological effects of unresolved guilt are the exact opposite of those of love. Unresolved guilt produces internal distress and anxiety. The stress related illnesses of high blood pressure, stomach ulcers, migraine headaches, ulcerative colitis and rheumatoid arthritis, if not caused by, can be significantly aggravated by the presence of, unresolved guilt. One's own immune system is suppressed in the presence of unresolved guilt. Immunosuppression increases the rate and incidence of infections and reduces one's ability to fight cancer. Unresolved guilt is capable of killing you!

42. Fox

What happiness for those whose guilt has been forgiven! What joys when sins are covered over! What relief for those who have confessed their sins and God has cleared their record. PSALM 32:1-2 TLB

Of course, as in all things regarding humans, every individual has a variable response depending upon a combination of one's own genetic and environmental factors. If one's own heredity is a predisposing factor to an unresolved guilt-related illness, the introduction of the experience of unresolved guilt may precipitate the illness. I have treated many such illnesses with modern effective medicines. I have, however, been impressed that if the underlying cause of the illness is unresolved guilt, modern medicine provides an often times effective but only partial treatment. In such illnesses, the patient has frequent recurrences and slowly and incompletely responds to medicine which in the same illness devoid of an underlying guilt factor would be rapidly effective and curative.

Much as the internal yearning for love drives us to search for God, the internal distress of guilt drives us to seek resolution through forgiveness. I have only found one mechanism by which we can believably and understandably resolve guilt. God provided that miraculous mechanism in allowing His Son to die for our sins. The crucifixion of Jesus 2,000 years ago stands as our mechanism to resolve the guilt we experience resulting from our wrongdoings. The day and time of His crucifixion mark the actual point in history which we can refer to as an offering by God to absolve our individual guilt. He allowed His Son to take all of our sins and wrongdoings to His cross of crucifixion.

I once thought all this to be nothing more than religious rhetoric—my sins nailed to the cross of Christ? In an unnatural world, survival depends on the accomplishment of the here and now. Our forgiveness is based on an event that has already happened and which predates both our sin and our guilt. It would be equivalent to a child realizing the affections of his heart would be satisfied by a certain Christmas gift ten minutes before the celebration of opening presents. There was not enough time to tell his parents of the desire of his heart. He opens his Christmas present and finds the very gift that he was considering not more than ten minutes ago. He then finds out that his parents had purchased the gift two weeks before Christmas based on their knowledge of his desires and for their love in wanting to provide for him the affections of his heart. Our forgiveness is given to us as a gift, as a result of an event that happened 2,000 years ago provided by God long before we had a realization of our necessity for the gift. But since God knows the desires of our hearts and minds, He had foreseen our coming necessity for a means of resolving guilt through His forgiveness.

43. MUSHROOMS

And you hath He quickened, who were dead in trespasses and sins; …And hath raised us up together in heavenly places in Christ Jesus. EPHESIANS 2:1,6 KJV

It was through what his Son did that God cleared a path for everything to come to Him— all things in heaven and on earth—for Christ's death on the cross has made peace with God for all by his blood. This includes you who were once so far away from God. You were His enemies and hated Him and were separated from Him by your evil thoughts and actions, Yet now, He has brought you back as His friends. He has done this through the death on the cross of His own human body and now as a result Christ has brought you into the very presence of God and you are standing there before Him with nothing left against you—nothing left that He could even chide you for, the only condition is that you fully believe the truth standing in it steadfast and firm, strong in the Lord, convinced of the good news that Jesus died for you and never shifting from trusting Him to save you. This is the wonderful news that came to each of you and is now spreading all over the world and I, Paul, have the joy of telling it to others.

Colossians 1:20-23 TLB

Many of us seek resolution of guilt from other people. Some equate resolution of guilt with acceptance and reinforcement from others. Many seek resolution of guilt by psychological defense mechanisms such as suppression of knowledge, denial of reality, and escape from reality by mind altering drugs; all of which lead to mental, emotional, spiritual and physical distress and afflictions. Many are then easily focused on the affliction and its manifestations but fail to address the underlying cause. An analogy would be to treat the symptoms of redness, swelling, heat and pus in tissues caused by an imbedded wood sliver without removing the sliver.

So then how are we to take advantage of this gift of forgiveness and absolution of guilt? For many it is too easy, all one has to do is believe that Jesus died for him or her. Just as love follows a belief in the life of Christ, forgiveness follows a belief in the death of Christ. It takes only faith— to believe. God's favor has always been won in a singular fashion—faith.

For the Scriptures tell us, Abraham believed God and that is why God canceled his sins and declared him not guilty. But didn't he earn his right to heaven by all the good things he did? No, for by being saved is a gift. If a person could earn it by being good, then it would not be free. But it is. It is given to those who do not work for it for God declares sinners to be good in his sight if they have faith in Christ to save them from God's wrath. *Romans 4:3-5 TLB*

44. FAWN

Noah found grace in the eyes of the Lord! GENESIS 6:8 KJV

What we see in and around us reveals God to us but has little to do with faith. True faith originates from that which cannot be seen. God places a premium on an attitude or state of mind which is based on faith. Where does faith come from?

So, faith comes from hearing, and hearing by the Word of Christ. ROMANS 10:13 NAS

Faith comes from listening. Faith comes from hearing His Word. God does not expect us to have a blind, senseless faith. He gives us His recorded Word upon which to base our faith. This gives great importance to the substance of His Word. But more importantly, it establishes the pre-eminence of His Son Christ. God's Word from the start to the end points the listener to the Cross of Christ. All roads and all pathways in the Bible lead to and intersect at the Cross. Why? Because in Christ there is all of God, and all of the Word.

And the Word became flesh, and dwelt among us, and beheld His glory, glory as of the only begotten from the Father, full of grace and truth. JOHN 1:14 NAS

Our greatest needs in life are to be found at the foot of the Cross of Christ: unconditional love and forgiveness, (and yet to be explained eternal life).

Now look out! Complete and total absolution of guilt leads to great joy and peace of mind. Since this state is not accomplished through great struggle, strife, exhaustion, and energy, it is contrary to the mind of the world. I have seen personal disbelief foil a person's individual accomplishment of forgiveness, but as often I have seen the jealousy of others lead to hesitation, doubt and disbelief as if the truth had become entangled in a web of confusion. The unforgiven seem to resent the joy and fulfillment of the forgiven. Once belief has enabled a person to grasp this mechanism, it must be protected by the strength and reinforcement of the faithful and forgiven, as well as the individual's own focus on the truth in the Word.

You were dead in sins and your sinful desires were not yet cut away. Then He gave you a share in the very life of Christ, for He forgave all your sins, and blotted out the charges proved against you, and the list of his commandments which you had not obeyed. He took this list of sins and destroyed it by nailing it to Christ's cross. In this way God took away satan's power to accuse you of sin and God openly displayed to the whole world Christ's triumph at the cross where your sins were all taken away. COLOSSIANS 2:13-15 TLB

45. COCK

"Peter," Jesus said, "before the cock crows a second time tomorrow morning you will deny me three times."
MARK 14:30 TLB

Don't let others spoil your faith and joy with their philosophies, their wrong and shallow answers built on men's thoughts and ideas instead of on what Christ has said.
COLOSSIANS 2:8 TLB

Just as an individual must experience unconditional love before they can give it, the individual must also experience forgiveness in order to give it. Next to guilt which results from a lack of absolution and forgiveness, resentment is detrimental. Resentment arises from the inability to forgive. Unresolved resentment carries with it the identical myriad of negative, detrimental and self-destructive emotional and physical consequences as does guilt. To carry resentment toward another is to inflict pain and suffering on one's self. The ability for an individual to forgive represents his mechanism to resolve resentment. To be able to live without resentment represents a gift of peace of mind, health, and fulfillment. Just as God's provision has enabled us a mechanism by which to obtain individual forgiveness, it is also His provision to enable us then to forgive others.

The full impact and reality of the love and forgiveness of Christ did not hit me until I was physically standing in Jerusalem. Judy and I were on a tour of the Holy Lands. I was standing in the court yard of the High Priest where Jesus was taken the night of his betrayal and capture. Just prior to his capture, He had been talking to his faithfully loyal and loving disciple, Peter. Peter was in disbelief and personally angered and repulsed at the thought of anyone betraying his beloved Jesus. Then Jesus told him that he, Peter, would deny Him, Jesus, three times before the cock crows the second time before sunrise that next morning.

"All of you will desert me," Jesus told them, "for God has declared through the prophets, I will kill the shepherd and the sheep will scatter. But after I am raised to life again, I will go to Galilee and meet you there." Peter said to Him, "I will never desert you no matter what the others do!" "Peter," Jesus said, "before the cock crows a second time tomorrow morning you will deny me three times." "No!" Peter exploded. "Not even if I have to die with you! I will never deny you!" MARK 14:27-31 TLB

Peter with one other of his disciple friends was admitted into the courtyard where Jesus was being held. The physical layout of this happening is most important to appreciate its full meaning. The court yard is small in physical size. The locations where Peter went on to deny that he knew Jesus were within full view and earshot of where Jesus was held. So not only did Peter explain to

46. Shepherd Feeding Sheep

Jesus said, "Then feed My sheep...." JOHN 21:17 TLB

"I AM the good shepherd; the good shepherd lays down His life for the sheep." JOHN 10:11 TLB

his questioners on three occasions that night that he did not know Jesus, but his denials would have been in full view and in earshot of Jesus. Oh how miserable Peter must have felt. Jesus probably saw and heard Peter reject and deny Him. He was so depressed and despondent and angry at himself that he fled the scene immediately. He went home to Galilee and resumed his vocation of fishing. After the resurrection of Christ, Jesus personally went to Peter on the shore of the sea of Galilee and asked him three times "if he loved Him" Jesus was so forgiving and loving that he gave Peter an equal number of opportunities to reinstate himself with Jesus to the number of occasions he denied Jesus. After each time Jesus asked Peter "if he loved Him," Jesus went on to command him to life's service in caring for his sheep. I am sure Peter would have been useful to Jesus before this circumstance; but how much more now could Peter speak of the love and forgiveness of Jesus. He had not only an intellectual knowledge of this love and forgiveness but he had an experiential knowledge of the fullness and completeness of the love and forgiveness of Christ.

After breakfast Jesus said to Simon Peter. "Simon, son of John, do you love me more than these others?" "Yes," Peter replied, "you know I am your friend." "Then feed my lambs," Jesus told him. Jesus repeated the question "Simon, son of John, do you really love me." "Yes, Lord," Peter said, "you know I am your friend." "Then care for my sheep," Jesus said. Once more He asked him, "Simon son of John, are you even my friend." Peter was grieved at the way Jesus asked the question this third time. "Lord, you know my heart, you know I am," he said. Jesus said, "then feed my sheep."
JOHN 21:15-17 TLB

Boy, I thought as I stood there reading this account in the Bible that same love and forgiveness is available to me right here and now. At that moment I experienced the magnitude of the love and forgiveness of Jesus. I had read those verses on many occasions in the past and had believed the content of these verses, but I guess I had never had faith in their substance for myself. My hope is that in the experience of reading this book you may develop this same faith.

But in contrast, consider Judas. On the same night he also betrayed Jesus. He identified Jesus to His captors. A no more severe offense than Peter's denial of Jesus. But what a contrast in outcome. Judas, severely stricken by guilt, took His own life. But, what a difference when forgiveness is granted and accepted . Filled with Christ's love and forgiveness, Peter goes on to accomplish a life's service to others in telling of the Gospel Message—the Good News of Christ.

47. FOOTPRINTS IN THE PARK

Jesus said, "I will not abandon you or leave you as orphans in the storm—I will come to you." JOHN 14:18 TLB

11 • The Christmas Gift and Eternal Life

Now, for the third and final part of the gift of Christmas—the resurrection of Jesus. After Jesus' life and death, He arose from the dead. He came back to life to live with His Father in heaven in both body and spirit for eternity. Did the resurrection of Christ actually happen?

> Indeed, taking all the evidence together, it is not too much to say that there is no historic incident better or more variously supported than the resurrection of Christ.
>
> –B. F. Westcott

> The fact of His resurrection is the most important event of history and therefore, appropriately, is one of the most certain facts in all history. Jesus not only predicted His death, but He also predicted His bodily resurrection. In John 2:19 He says, "Destroy this temple, and in three days I will raise it up." Here, temple refers to His body.
>
> –Henry Morris

It took His death to transform our spirit into perfection. It took His resurrection to transform our physical bodies into perfection.

48. CAVE

And the angel answered and said to the woman, "He is not here, for He is risen…" MATTHEW 28:6 KJV

The resurrection of Christ is the seal of our resurrection. The healing of sick people does not warrant us in believing that Christ will heal each of us today. Nor did the resurrection of Lazarus guarantee our immortality. It is the resurrection of Christ as firstfruits which alone opens the grave—in anticipation—to the believer and unto life eternal. Because He rose, we shall rise. [Romans 8:11]

–Ramm

You see, after His own physical resurrection, He made it possible for our own physical bodies to one day be transformed and perfected to unite with our perfected spirits in heaven.

I was initially impressed that the apostle Paul had reasoned that after his conversion in order to develop greater understanding of Jesus he returned to the places where Jesus walked, talked, and lived. He befriended those closest to Jesus in order to obtain his own personal knowledge of Jesus. Being naturally minded, I reasoned that even in modern times the same could be accomplished.

Judy and I traveled to Israel to retrace the life and times of the Biblical Jesus to see for ourselves the remnants of these events, the lay of the land, and the nature of the people. The most significant and inspiring event occurred when we were allowed to enter the small tomb of Jesus. To see and be in the very presence of the slab of rock upon which was carved a depression for the head of Jesus and see the carved depression at the other end for the imprint of his heels was awesome. At that moment the most significant event and realization of the trip impressed itself upon my mind. My affections almost became reverent for this tomb. Then it hit me! There was something missing—it was Jesus! He was gone—the tomb was empty! The object of my affection and reverence was absent. He was actually gone from the tomb. I then realized that I had traveled half-way around the world to find a person who in this generation is not to be found in a tomb but in the hearts of mankind. But the experience more concretely impressed upon me, the truth of His teachings. That His Spirit would reside in the hearts of those who received Him and that He himself would arise after His death, leave the tomb and return to His Father in heaven.

No, I will not abandon you or leave you as orphans in the storm—I will come to you. In just a little while, I will be gone from the world, but I will still be present with you.
JOHN 14:18-19 TLB

I saw nothing in the physical presence of His tomb that would refute His claims. There I was standing in His tomb with the full knowledge and reassurance of His Spirit within my heart looking at an empty slab. He had returned to His Father. The same promise of destiny is offered to individuals who accept Him as their own gift—the promise of eternal life after death. Just as Jesus broke the chains of death holding Him to the unnatural world to ascend to heaven for eternal life, so we too are able to vacate the grave and go to heaven. God offers us the capability to leave an unnatural physical world of pain, suffering, distress, heartache and sorrow to ascend to a place of peace, harmony, love and perfection.

The Scriptures tell us that the first man, Adam, was given a natural, human body but Christ is more than that, for He was life-giving Spirit.

First, then, we have these human bodies, and later on God gives us spiritual, heavenly bodies. Adam was made from the dust of the earth, but Christ came from heaven above. Every human being has a body just like Adam's, made of dust, but all who become Christ's will have the same kind of body as His—a body from heaven. Just as each of us now has a body like Adam's, so we shall some day have a body like Christ's.

I tell you this, my brothers: an earthly body made of flesh and blood cannot get into God's kingdom. These perishable bodies of ours are not the right kind to live forever. But I am telling you this strange and wonderful secret: we shall not all die, but we shall all be given new bodies! It will all happen in a moment, in the twinkling of an eye, when the last trumpet is blown. For there will be a trumpet blast from the sky and all the Christians who have died will suddenly become alive, with new bodies that will never, never die; and then we who are still alive shall suddenly have new bodies too. For our earthly bodies, the ones we have now that can die, must be transformed into heavenly bodies that cannot perish but will live forever.

When that happens, then at last this Scripture will come true—"Death is swallowed up in victory." O death, where then your victory? Where then your sting? For sin—the sting that causes death—will all be gone; and the law, which reveals our sins, will no longer be our judge. How we thank God for all of this! It is He who makes us victorious through Jesus Christ our Lord!

So, my dear brothers, since future victory is sure, be strong and steady, always abounding in the Lord's work, for you know that nothing you do for the Lord is ever wasted as it would be if there were no resurrection.

I CORINTHIANS 15:45-58 TLB

I will have to admit that to my natural mind this seems abstract. But to the spiritual mind it makes perfect sense. Both our spirits and our physical bodies will some day be made perfect. This is the "blessed hope" for believers. (Titus 2:13)

God created mankind in the form of Adam. He existed in peace, perfection and harmony with God. Then as an act of his own free will, he disobeyed God. At that point in the history of God's creation, the peace, perfection, and harmony of the universe became temporarily separated from the life and creation of mankind. Humans became separated from God. This one man's disobedience brought death to the universe and to us.

But God gives us a second chance to accomplish peace, perfection, and harmony with Him. Just as it was through the individual act of Adam's free will to separate us from God, so too it is through the act of our own free will to accept His Son as our Redeemer and Savior to rejoin us with God. At salvation we take in the very mind of Christ.

But strange as it seems, we Christians actually do have within us a portion of the very thoughts and mind of Christ. I CORINTHIANS 2:16 TLB

It is the incorporation of the mind of Christ which completes and perfects our spirit. The willful acceptance of Christ bridges the gap between God's Spirit and our spirit which He imparted to us at our creation. Since Adam's disobedience, however, there has been a separation between the Spirit of God and God's Spirit in us. Even many physical scientists today conclude that there is a part of human life which transcends this physical world and like the universe itself goes on infinitely and eternally. Many conclude that it is our soul or spirit. The central question is where does it go? At physical death those whose spirits are joined with the mind of Christ by a salvation experience are reunited to eternal peace, perfection, and harmony with God in heaven. Those who have not experienced salvation through the acceptance of Christ, go into eternal misery. At physical death, man's spirit coupled with the mind of Christ, is reunited to peace, perfection, and harmony with God in heaven. During our physical life, we only see traces and glimpses of the potential perfection of physical human life. God has revealed this to modern science in many ways. Increasing evidence exists today which demonstrates the potential for the mind of individuals to reverse the process of aging, rid their bodies of infection, eradicate cancer cells within their bodies, and in general overcome disease and affliction.

I think the observation of these processes and potentials of the physical body are remnants of man's original state of physical perfection. They are the processes which were devised by God in order for us to maintain perfect health. Their presence does indeed demonstrate to us the physical strengths we can call into our battle against pain, suffering, and disease. But they are strengths which we will never be able to call into perfect action. Our physical bodies are unnaturally on a course of destruction. Thank God our spirits can accomplish immortality and eternal perfection through our union with Christ! For only then can our physical bodies be someday transformed into perfection and reunited with our spirits in eternity.

The possibility of obtaining this perfect state of physical well-being and health through earthly awareness and consciousness, or through meditation to a higher level of consciousness, is a deception! God has only given us the ability through recent scientific technologies to see a glimpse of this possibility for ourselves in order to reveal more of Himself and His nature to us. God's only plan for imparting this peace, perfection, and harmony of well-being and health to be experienced by us is by our own salvation and redemption through His Son on the cross. This then ensures the believer not of perfection in our physical life, but perfection in our infinite and immortal spiritual life and in eternal life after death.

The only promise of perfect mental, emotional, spiritual, and physical health to mankind is to be realized through faith. You see, after an individual experiences salvation by accepting Christ and becomes obedient to God's Will, all that happens is assuredly for their own personal and God's ultimate good. In the state of submission of our own will to the Will of God, there is total security, serenity, peace, and perfection. The body, soul, and spirit are all in harmony. This state is unaffected by illness or health, success or failure, riches or poverty, and life or death. No matter what happens or what the circumstance, God's Will will be done. Eternal life has already been accomplished by salvation so what else matters? This position is gained through personal faith in the ultimate authority and personal submission to God's Will for your life. This position once gained cannot be lost and is not affected by personal performance. It is offered by the grace of God and cannot be won or achieved but can only be accepted as a personal gift from God by faith. It is the most personally secure valued position on planet earth. The rewards of the position are the personal realities of the fruits of the Holy Spirit; love, joy, peace, patience, kindness, goodness, faithfulness, gentleness and self control.

The same heavenly state of peace and harmony can indeed be accomplished in this physical world in a spiritual sense. For Jesus taught that after we receive Him into our hearts while on earth we are able to experience His perfection from within. But before we can be filled with God's perfection in Spirit, we have to experience personal brokenness and emptiness. The pathway to this position is often gained through personal pain, suffering, and sacrifice. It is not a journey for the faint-hearted. Its entrance requires a breaking of one's own person. The fullness of God can only be approached from a personal state of weakness and emptiness.

Paul also taught that this state of perfection could be accomplished within:

But this precious treasure—this light and power that now shines within us—is held in a perishable container, that is, in our weak bodies. Everyone can see that the glorious power within must be from God and is not our own. We are pressed on every side by troubles, but not crushed and broken. We are perplexed but we don't know why things happen as they do, but we don't give up and quit. We are hunted down, but God never abandons us. We get knocked down, but we get up again and keep going. These bodies of ours are constantly facing death just as Jesus did; so it is clear to all that it is only the living Christ within who [keeps us safe]. II CORINTHIANS 4:7-10 TLB

49. HEAVEN

Jesus answered, "Let not your hearts be troubled, you believe in God, believe also in Me. In my Father's house are many mansions; If it were not so I would have told you; I go to prepare a place for you. And if I go and prepare a place for you, I will come again and receive you unto myself; that where I AM, there you may be also. JOHN 14:1-3 KJV

12 • Observations of Heaven

I have been privileged to attend many a sick and dying patient at their bedsides during their last moments of life. I have never seen heaven with my own eyes. My only glimpse of heaven has been through the dying patient's thoughts, feelings and attitudes; and my own experiences of receiving and enjoying the reality of the fruits of the Holy Spirit. I have been enlightened and humbled by the grace, courage, love, peace, dignity, and faith of the many who have died before my eyes knowing their destiny to be heaven.

I have observed that in great measure the peace and expectation of the dying has its foundation in an anticipated reunion with loved ones—a parent reunited with a child, a child with a parent, a husband awaiting a reunion with his wife, a wife with her husband. For many faithful it is the expected reunion with Jesus Himself which sustains them through to the end. These are all comforting and reassuring thoughts; but it has been my observation that thoughts without substance flee especially in the face of pain, suffering, sacrifice, and death. These thoughts are steadfast to the faithful! God has provided to the

50. RUSHING RIVER

And he showed me a river of the water of life, clear as crystal, coming from the throne of God and of the Lamb, in the middle of its street. And on either side of the river was the tree of life. REVELATION 22:1-2 NAS

And He who sits on the throne said, "Behold, I AM making all things new." And He said, "Write, for these words are faithful and true." And He said to me, "It is done. I AM the Alpha and the Omega, the beginning and the end. I will give to the one who thirsts from the spring of the water of life without cost." REVELATION 21:5-6 NAS

faithful a mechanism to confirm and substantiate these promises. God's affirmation of their reality to the dying provides them the substance upon which they are founded. I have observed the dying adhere to these promises in the face of insurmountable human misery. I conclude, therefore, that these events and promises have a foundation of substance. God's heavenly provision for man is real.

Jesus answered, "Let not your heart be troubled. You are trusting God, now trust in me. There are many homes up there where my Father lives and I am going to prepare them for your coming. When everything is ready, then I will come and get you, so that you can always be with me where I am. If this were not so, I would tell you plainly. And you know where I am going and how to get there." JOHN 14:1-4 TLB

To those courageous people and their families who have allowed me to participate in this meaningful and sacred event in their lives, I owe a debt of gratitude. During this very private moment which represents their last hours and minutes in our unnatural world, I have found it comforting and faith building to observe their reassuring faith that they are *going home.* In fact, they are going home! Their physical bodies are con-

strained to the imperfections of this unnatural world. Their physical bodies are constrained to death in this world. Their spirits will escape this unnatural world and live in eternity with God in His perfect, natural world in heaven. Here also, in time, will their transformed physical bodies rejoin their spirits. During these last moments of life in the physical world, their faith in the existence of their eternal life most assuredly gives them an insight, a sense of reassurance, and a sense of expectation as they make their exit from this life. I can only conclude that during this time our loving and protecting God confers to the believer these affirmations while they maintain the last of their unnatural physical lives.

The evidence for this conclusion is based on my observations that, for the believer, this transition from physical life through death to eternal life is made without a spiritual struggle and in many cases with a sense of anticipation. I think it is a fitting tribute to make these observations and conclusions in honor of God's love for mankind. After all, He made a supreme sacrifice to insure a loving, peaceful, joyous spiritual life. It only follows with His nature that He would also provide us with a most peaceful, reassuring, spiritual victory over physical death. After all, physical death merely represents the unnatural end to our earthly life; even though at times physical death is preceded by physical sufferings.

These sufferings represent the aftermath of Adam's disobedience to God. Adam's choice turned a perfect, natural world of physical health into an unnatural physical world of disease, pain, and death. Therefore, I do not find it difficult to believe that an all-loving God would make such a provision for our death as He did for our life. The reality of death without faith is struggle, strife, and exhaustion. The faithful seem to endure death with ease, contentment, and peace. God grants to those who have Jesus, the powers which enables the believer to implement the physiology of faith, hope, and love in the fullness of life, but also to the end of life in death.

To one who is understandably focused on mankind's fulfillment of life and quality of death, I consider eternal life as a *signing bonus*. I can only imagine the existence of heaven because I know Jesus is not in His tomb, and I know Him to be a man of His Word, and I have experienced His Kingdom from within.

For Jesus answered and said, ... "For only I, the Messiah, have come to earth and will return to heaven again. And as Moses in the wilderness lifted up the bronze image of a serpent on a pole, even so I must be lifted up upon a pole, so that anyone who believes in me will have eternal life. For God loved the world so much that He gave his only Son so that anyone who believes in Him shall not perish but have eternal life. God did not send his Son into the world to condemn it but to save it."
JOHN 3:13-17 TLB

I can only imagine the reality of the peace and presence of heaven as I have seen through the eyes of the dying believer.

Our only duty is to receive this gift so that we in turn are capable of giving the gift. The more we give the more we receive. Regardless of a person's age, conduct, position, or circumstance in life, the gift is equally available to all. God has promised us that from the anticipation and innocence of youth to the integrity and endurance of old age, His gift is awaiting our receipt.

...And to him who knocks it shall be opened. LUKE 11:10 NAS

For there is no distinction between Jew and Greek; for the same Lord is Lord of all, abounding in riches for all who call upon Him.

ROMANS 9:12 NAS

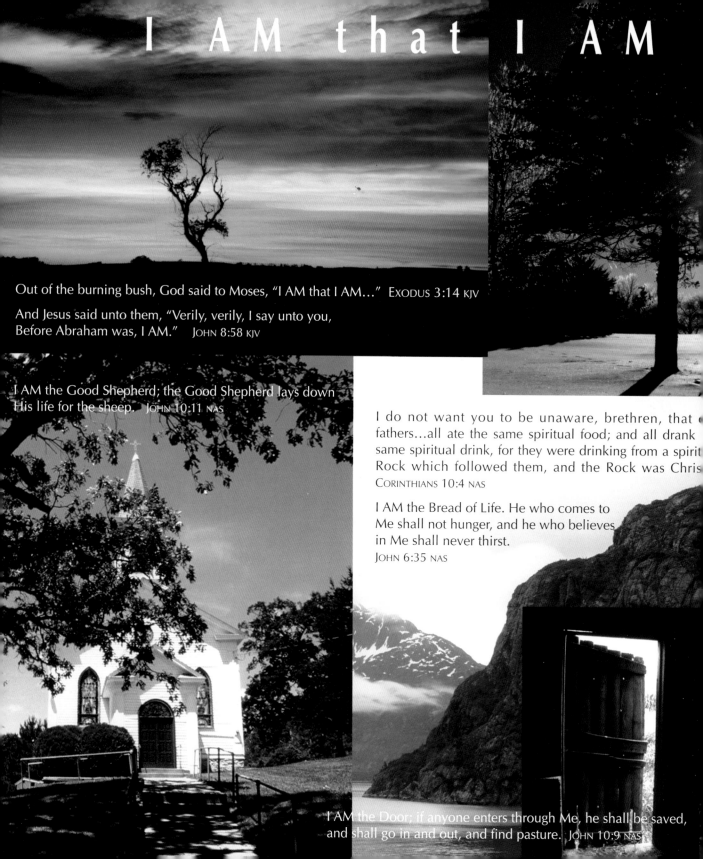

I AM that I AM

Out of the burning bush, God said to Moses, "I AM that I AM…" EXODUS 3:14 KJV

And Jesus said unto them, "Verily, verily, I say unto you, Before Abraham was, I AM." JOHN 8:58 KJV

I AM the Good Shepherd; the Good Shepherd lays down His life for the sheep. JOHN 10:11 NAS

I do not want you to be unaware, brethren, that ‹ fathers…all ate the same spiritual food; and all drank same spiritual drink, for they were drinking from a spirit Rock which followed them, and the Rock was Chris‹ CORINTHIANS 10:4 NAS

I AM the Bread of Life. He who comes to Me shall not hunger, and he who believes in Me shall never thirst. JOHN 6:35 NAS

I AM the Door; if anyone enters through Me, he shall be saved, and shall go in and out, and find pasture. JOHN 10:9 NAS

I AM the Lord. And the blood shall be a sign for you on the houses where you live; and when I see the blood I will pass over you. EXODUS 12:12,13 NAS

I AM the Resurrection and the Life; He who believes in Me shall live even if he dies. JOHN 11:25 NAS

I AM the Light of the World. He who follows Me shall not walk in darkness, but shall have the Light of Life. JOHN 8:12 NAS

I AM the Vine, you are the branches. He that abideth in Me, and I in him, the same bringeth forth much fruit; for without Me you can do nothing. JOHN 15:5 KJV

He who sits on the throne said, "Behold, ...I AM the Alpha and the Omega, the beginning and the end. I will give to the one who thirsts from the spring of the water of life without cost." REVELATION 21:5,6 NAS

I AM the Way, the Truth, and the Life: no man cometh unto the Father, but through Me. JOHN 14:6 KJV

51. BUCK

Pride goeth before destruction, and a haughty spirit before a fall. PROVERBS 16:18 *KJV*

13 • Receiving the Christmas Gift

Well, how do we receive this gift? There is nothing we can do to earn the right of receiving this gift. If that were the case, it would not be a true gift (free). Being religious and bound to religious rituals has nothing to do with receiving this gift, except to possibly act as a barrier:

> These rules may seem good, for rules of this kind require strong devotion and are humiliating and hard on the body, but they have no effect when it comes to conquering a person's evil thoughts and desires. They only make him proud. COLOSSIANS 2:23 TLB

According to Proverbs 6:16-19, pride is the most despised of human qualities by God. Why? Because pride separates man from God. The prideful religious think that they have received God, but all they have is formality and rituals of religion. Sadly, they often do not have a relationship with God, because they have been so preoccupied with their religious activities that they have missed the Person of God, they have missed the gift! But there are many other sources of pride which act as a barrier to our receiving God. Often times it is our strongest personal

52. TURKEY

The Scripture says, "God is opposed to the proud, But gives grace to the humble." JAMES 4:6 NAS

attribute which acts as a barrier to our receiving God. If a person is extremely intellectual, it will be easy for them to think of themselves too smart to need God. After all, they can think their way out of their shortcomings. If a person is extremely wealthy, it will be easy for them to think themselves too rich and too secure to need God. After all, they can buy their way out of their shortcomings. For whatever the specific reason, the one thing common to the prideful is an over-estimation of their own value. They think of themselves as so valuable that they are automatic shoo-ins for God. After all, how could God not be overly moved and impressed with their stature? But their way to receive the gift is no different than any one else's.

At the other end of the spectrum are those who think so lowly of themselves that they conclude that they are unacceptable to God. Nothing could be further from the truth. God comes to man in his weakness, not in his strength. When we are strong, we conclude that we do not need God. When we are weak, we realize our deprivation as a human and, therefore, our need for God. We look outside of ourselves more easily when we know ourselves to be weak. When we are strong, we look only to ourselves and, therefore, miss God. No one is too weak to receive God. He has no standards of conduct or levels of accomplishment as a prerequisite to offering humans His gift. He comes to us in whatever circumstance leads us to look for Him.

The only thing we can do to insure our receipt of the gift is to recognize our need for it. In other words, recognize one's own individual need for Jesus in one's life. In order to see oneself in need of Jesus, one must not see oneself as being ideal or perfect. For that individual has no need for goodness, for by their own estimation they are already good and have no need for God. No, rather we must see ourselves as we really are—as God sees us. Many great and accomplished people have stated that their most difficult and painful task in life has been to see themselves as they really are. One must see that as a human in general and as an individual in specific their nature is in need of a dose of goodness and love. We must see that by ourselves and by our own merits that we are inadequate. When we have attained this fundamental truthful assessment of our own inadequacies and deficiencies, we are ready for the opportunity to accept the gift of Jesus—only because we have seen our own need. To receive the gift, it takes no more planning, work or effort than it did for us to experience our physical birth. The only difference is

53. HUMMINGBIRD

Most gladly therefore will I rather glory in my infirmities, that the power of Christ may rest upon us...
For when I am weak, then am I strong. II CORINTHIANS 12:9-10 KJV

that the receipt of this gift is a conscious choice. In God's loving kindness for us, He gave us a free will by which to either accept His gift or reject His gift. God's love is not forceful or demanding.

Now, when need intersects with opportunity, the equation is complete. In order to accept and receive His gift, all one has to do is open His heart as a child and say "yes, I see" and "yes, I believe" that you sent your Son as my gift so that I might receive Him into my heart.

Jesus said, "Let the little children come to me, for the Kingdom of God belongs to such as they. Don't send them away. I tell you as seriously as I know how that anyone who refuses to come to God as a little child will never be allowed into His Kingdom." MARK 10:14-15 TLB

Why is it important to actually say a Sinner's Prayer?

For salvation that comes from trusting Christ, which is what we preach, is already within easy reach of each of us. In fact, it is as near as our own hearts and mouths. For, if you tell others with your own mouth that Jesus Christ is your Lord and believe in your own heart that God has raised him from the dead, you will be saved. For it is by believing in his heart that a man becomes right with God and, with his mouth he tells others of his faith confirming his salvation. For the Scriptures tell us that no one who believes in Christ will ever be disappointed. Jew and Gentile are the same in this respect. They all have the same Lord who generously gives His riches to all those who ask Him for them. Anyone who calls upon the name of the Lord will be saved. ROMANS 10:8-13 TLB

Allow me to put it in my own words. Image that you generally don't feel well. You are experiencing nothing specific, only general symptoms. There may be no physical signs of your disease on your outside. After your condition is evaluated and assessed you are presented with the evidence that you have sugar diabetes. The characteristics and presentation of man's spiritual illness is often similar. The individual person senses that things are not all well on their inside or in their life, but do not know what is really wrong. Everything on the outside of their life may appear to be acceptable and normal. If there are outside visible clues and signs of an illness, they are often denied and rationalized away. This denial and rationalization process is common in all kinds of physical illnesses and is specifically common with regard to our spiritual illnesses. But some circumstance, situation, or more often the person's own conscience, accuses them and

54. Kool Aid Stand

Jesus said, "Let the little children come unto Me, for the Kingdom of God belongs to such as they. Don't send them away! I tell you as seriously as I know how that anyone who refuses to come to God as a little child will never be allowed into His Kingdom." MARK 10:14-15 TLB

convicts them of their own spiritual illness and condition.

> *...He will punish the heathen when they sin, even though they never had God's written laws, for down in their hearts they know right from wrong. God's laws are written within them, their own conscience accuses them; or sometimes excuses them.* ROMANS 2:12-15 TLB

The operation of the conscience causes internal distress. This internal distress causes an individual to consider and seek a solution to this state of internal distress and discomfort.

Once the diagnosis is evidenced and accepted by the individual with diabetes or with a spiritual illness, treatment can begin. The treatment for diabetes involves taking insulin (or medication). The treatment of the diabetic commences with a choice and a commitment to take insulin. A prescription for insulin can be taken to the pharmacy, discussed with the pharmacist, talked about with others, theorized and conjectured about, but is of no effect until it is taken in by the individual. The person will not be on the road to health and recovery until the insulin is taken into the physical body.

The same is true for the acceptance and the taking in of Christ for the treatment of our spiritual illness and condition. Like diabetes, man's spiritual separation from God and deprivation of our spirit is not superficial, like a skin disease. Therefore the application of a salve, cream, or ointment to cover the outside will have no effect on our spiritual illness just as it would have no effect on an individual's illness of diabetes. Like the injection of insulin for the diabetic, the Person and Spirit of Christ must be taken into the body for the spiritually ill.

Similar to the individual administration of insulin as an injection into the body, a personal administration of Christ must start with an individual decision and choice of commitment to receive Christ into one's own self. This personal injection of Christ into one's self is the treatment. As insulin is absorbed into the veins and arteries of the body, it then disseminates throughout the systems, organs and tissues of the body where it begins to transform the entire body by bonding to each cell in the body.

The same is true for the infusion of Christ through one's mind into the entire body. Christ fully disseminates throughout the body to the depth of the marrow of the bones, through to the very depth of the spirit of man. When His Spirit bonds with our spirit, there is formed a new person with a set of new characteristics common to

55. CHURCH

For where two or three have gathered together in My name, there I AM in their midst. MATTHEW 18:20 NAS

those of Christ. The same is true for the newly diagnosed diabetic after treatment is initiated. I have heard it said many times, "I feel like a new person."

Unlike diabetes, where there is no instant cure, Christ is the instant cure for our spiritual disease of sin. Unlike the diabetic who is required to daily manage his disease with insulin for the rest of his life, the newborn Christian having taken in Christ is instantly cured of his spiritual disease. Man's spiritual affliction, unlike that of the diabetic's, is a curable disease.

The diabetic becomes an expert in his disease through the power of knowledge. The knowledge of his disease is acquired from support groups, activities and education, personal education, and through the development of personal alliances and friendships with those who also have diabetes. The same is true for the life-long growth and development of the new person in Christ. Liberation from the effects of the old person comes through knowledge of His Word and Will.

My people are destroyed for lack of knowledge.
HOSEA 4:6

The individual with Christ will be strengthened, educated, and personally supported by a church group, a personal pastor, personal time in God's Word, personal time in prayer, and through the development of loving, meaningful, lasting Christ-centered friendships. But most importantly through an intimate, personal, lasting relationship with the very Person of Christ.

If you are willing to acknowledge your spiritual condition and sinful nature which has become separated from God, the equation is complete. Opportunity at this moment is intersecting with need. If you choose to receive Christ as your Lord and Savior you can do it now! At this moment you can either bow your head or get on your knees and say the sinner's prayer:

Oh God, I need your help, your love, and your forgiveness. I need you in my life. I am a sinner. I ask and receive your Son Jesus into my life; as my Savior from my sins, and as my Lord, to direct and guide me in my life. God, please direct me into your Will for my life through your Son, your Word, and your Holy Spirit. I thank you in Jesus' name. Amen.

❄

Congratulations.

You have identified and treated your spiritual disease and are cured! Now you are instructed to tell others. You are also instructed to follow Christ in all things, including baptism.

56. Bird Nest

Jesus replied, "...Men can only produce human life, but the Holy Spirit gives new life from heaven; so don't be surprised at my statement that you must be born again!" JOHN 3:6,7 TLB

And Jesus arrived from Galilee at the Jordan coming to John to be baptized by him. And after being baptized, Jesus went up immediately from the water; and behold, the heavens were opened and He saw the Spirit of God descending as a dove, and coming upon Him, and behold, a voice out of the heavens, saying, "This is My beloved Son, in Whom I am well pleased." MATTHEW 3:13,16,17 NAS

The Spirit of God descends upon those whose actions are in submission to, and obedient to, God. Why does God instruct us to do these things? Only God knows from the inside the changed status of your spirit. His knowledge is of supreme importance. But, He is pleased by your actions of obedience because they are an outward demonstration of your faith. He desires your faith to be seen by others. Your obedience to His instructions, demonstrated by your outward actions, is the evidence to others of your faith. You are instructed not to hide your faith but to show it to others. He is the Light of the world. If you hide a candle, the light grows dim. Your faith is the evidence of His Light in your life and in the world—let it shine brightly!.

Ye are the light of the world, a city that is set on a hill cannot be hid. Neither do men light a candle, and put it under a bushel, but on a candlestick; and it giveth light unto all that are in the house. Let your light so shine before men, that they may see your good works, and glorify your Father which is in heaven. MATTHEW 5:14-16 KJV

Through this individual act of the human will, you have literally caused a biological and physiological change in your physical body, mind, emotions, and spirit. The impetus for this change begins with the action of the human will. When the human willfully commits to change, that change becomes a reality. When activated and fueled by the willful taking in of the Person of Christ (the very mind of Christ), and sustained by the power of human faith, change becomes a reality. A willful committed faith in Christ, energized by the actual presence of His person in you, is the catalyst which not only initiates, but also sustains, this biochemical conversion of the body, soul, and spirit—this is a life-changing event if you faithfully will it to be.

Through your acceptance of Christ you have accessed and taken in the very mind of Christ and God. Your mind, your thoughts, your emotions, and your attitudes will now be guided by the presence of the indwelling Holy Spirit. In so doing, you now have all of God inside you. As a human, you now have a new nature. You have been born again. Not a physical birth, you have already accomplished that on your birthday, but a spiritual birth. Your new spirit is now the spirit of Jesus. You have willfully taken Jesus into your own heart. You have received the true gift of Christmas.

> *Jesus replied, "With all the earnestness that I possess I tell you this, unless you are born again you can never enter into the kingdom of God."* *"Born again" exclaimed Nicodemus, "what do you mean? How can an old man go back into his mother's womb and be born again?" Jesus replied, "What I am telling you so earnestly is this, unless one is born of water and the spirit, he cannot enter the kingdom of God. Men can only reproduce human life but the Holy Spirit gives new life from heaven. So don't be surprised at my statement that you must be born again."* JOHN 3:3-7 TLB

Just as we are born into a human family, as in the unnatural world, God has made a provision for our spiritual birth into His own family.

> *His unchanging plan has always been to adopt us into His own family by sending Jesus Christ to die for us and He did this because He wanted to.* EPHESIANS 1:5 TLB

Now that His Spirit has been incorporated into our hearts, He is capable of utilizing the same anatomy and physiology and the same innate patterns of thought and action to transform the heartache and misery of guilt, jealousy, envy, anger, spite, hostility, and madness with that of love. Consider this:

> *You are living a brand new kind of life that is continually learning more and more of what is right and trying constantly to be more and more like Christ who created this new life within you. In this new life, one's nationality or race or education or social position is unimportant, such things mean nothing. Whether a person has Christ is what matters and he is equally available to all.* COLOSSIANS 3:10-11 TLB

New Life

57. Tree By the River

And he shall be like a tree planted by the rivers of water, that bringeth forth his fruit in his season; his leaf also shall not wither; and whatsoever he doeth shall prosper. PSALM 1:3 KJV

14 ◆ New Life Takes Root

Be patient! Over time your life has taken on the characteristics of sin. So too, will your new nature and new life need time to become shaped, molded, conformed, and transformed into that which will eventually fulfill God's purpose for you. You are a new house—under construction!

As a human, you were predestined to take on and develop certain of your families' characteristics, manners, and pattern of thought and action. Now, as a newborn Christian, you are encouraged to join into your new family. The Christian family is the church. Through the fellowship and friendship of other Christians in the church, and through the instructions and teachings of the pastor, you will take on the characteristics of the Head of the church—Jesus. Remember, you are now the House of the Lord—under construction! Of vital importance is that you build your Christian character on a solid foundation. A foundation of Biblical teaching and training.

All who listen to my instructions and follow them are wise, like a man who builds his house on solid rock. Though the rain comes in torrents,

58. Footprints in the Snow

And Jesus said, "I will not leave you comfortless: I will come to you." JOHN 14:18 KJV

and the floods rise and the storm winds beat against his house, it won't collapse, for it is built on rock.

But those who hear my instructions and ignore them are foolish, like a man who builds his house on sand. For when the rains and floods come, and storm winds beat against his house, it will fall with a mighty crash." The crowds were amazed at Jesus' sermons, for He taught as one who had great authority, and not as their Jewish leaders. MATTHEW 7:24-28 TLB

The only constant in this tumultuous physical unnatural life is God. God is the Word. The consistency and solidarity of your foundation depends upon your individual faith and commitment to God, His church, and His Word.

Through this state of spiritual acceptance and harmony with God, you are capable of escaping the bounds of your physical pain and suffering and eventually your own physical death. Just as Jesus was raised from His physical death to heaven, so too will your individual Spirit, and in time your physical body, ascend to heaven after your physical death.

And Jesus said, "For only I, the Messiah, have come to earth and will return to heaven again. And as Moses in the wilderness lifted up the bronze image of a serpent on a pole, even so I must be lifted up upon a pole so that anyone who believes in me will have eternal life. For God loved the world so much that He gave his only Son so that anyone who believes in Him shall not perish but have eternal life. God did not send his Son to the world to condemn it but to save it." JOHN 3:13-17 TLB

But in the meantime your physical state as well as your spiritual state can be energized and healed through the operation of faith, hope, and love. You will never be alone. Even in the depth of darkness and cold of your circumstance or situation, you will be preceded by your companion, Jesus. With true faith you will be able to see His footprints preceding you and sense His presence. From the innocence and vigor of youth to the weathered wisdom of age, you are never alone. You have activated your ability to love not only God, but also other individuals. God intends for this power to provide not just good thoughts but also good actions.

It is through the love and forgiveness of others that the inner fulfillment of life is accomplished. Many great people of medicine have recognized and realized the beneficial effects on oneself as a result of helping others. Dr. Normal Sheely, an internationally known neurosurgeon and pioneer

59. SHEPHERDING NEW LIFE

For the whole law can be summed up in this one command: "Love others as you love yourself."
GALATIONS 5:14 TLB

in the treatment of chronic pain syndromes, states that it is essential for the benefit and recovery of the patient to have the ability to forgive, to obtain the ability to satisfy their individual need and desire to feel love, and to be able to exercise their desire and need to do good to others.

William Shakespeare put it this way:
It is one of the most beautiful compensations of this life that no man can sincerely try to help another without helping himself.

60. FAWN DRINKING

Jesus stood and cried out, saying, "If any man is thirsty, let him come to Me and drink. He who believes in Me, as the Scripture said, From his innermost being, shall flow rivers of living water." JOHN 7:37-38 NAS

15 • Living In the Spirit

It is through the ability to relate to others and one's self with love that God continues to reveal himself to the world and to individuals.

What does this have to do with the physical body and health? Well, it is often the circumstance that the body is unable to accomplish its phenomenal feats of healing until the spirit is healed. All illnesses do have a spiritual origin. The recovery from and treatment of all illnesses in some way can be affected by the state of the spirit of the afflicted individual. This principle can be seen in the following example:

> *Soon some men brought him a paralyzed boy on a mat. When Jesus saw their faith, he said to the sick boy, "Cheer up, son! For I have forgiven your sins!" "Blasphemy! This man is saying that he is God!" exclaims some of the religious leaders to themselves. Jesus knew what they were thinking and asked them, "Why are you thinking such evil thoughts? I, the Messiah, have the authority on earth to forgive sins. But talk is cheap—anybody could say that. So I will prove it to you by healing this man." Then turning to the paralyzed man, he commanded, "Pick up your stretcher and go home for you are healed." And the boy jumped up and left!* MATTHEW 9:2-7

61. Living Water

Now there came a woman of Samaria to draw water... Jesus said to her, "If you knew the gift of God, and who it is who says to you, 'Give me a drink,' you would have asked Him, and He would have given you living water." John 4:7,10 NAS

You see, God healed this paralytic boy's spirit before he concerned himself with his body. Jesus simply offered the boy forgiveness. His offering of forgiveness healed the boy's spiritual inadequacy and united the boy's spirit with the Spirit of God. We all as humans have that same spiritual inadequacy and illness, which separates us from the Spirit of God. Here is a boy who physically can't even walk, but Jesus himself first heals the boy's spirit by granting him forgiveness when his most obvious visible sufferings are physical. Why? Because Jesus came to heal the spiritually sick more so than the physically sick. Why? Because He knows that man's physical body is constrained to the realities of this physical world. The physical body will someday die. But He also knows that it is the spirit of man which has the capacity to live forever in eternity and from that perspective is much more vital and important. Because it is our spirit which precedes and predetermines that our transformed physical bodies will also reach perfection in eternity.

And the dust returns to the earth as it was and the spirit returns to God who gave it.
ECCLESIASTES 12:7

But God does not commit the believer's physical body only to eternal dust.

But our homeland is in heaven, where our Savior the Lord Jesus Christ is; and we are looking forward to His return from there. When He comes back He will take these dying bodies of ours and change them into glorious bodies like His own, using the same mighty power that He will use to conquer all else everywhere.
PHILIPPIANS 3:20-21 TLB

Paul taught the same principles to the Christians of his day:

That is why we never give up. Though our bodies are dying, our inner strength in the Lord is growing every day. These troubles and sufferings of ours are, after all, quite small and won't last very long. Yet this short time of distress will result in God's richest blessing upon us forever and ever! So we do not look at what we can see right now, the troubles all around us, but we look forward to the joys in heaven which we have not yet seen. The troubles will soon be over, but the joys to come will last forever.
II CORINTHIANS 4:16-18 TLB

He desires us to come to the same perspectives. After all, it is our spirit that God first wishes to communicate with and individually relate to not our physical body. But Jesus did not, however, forgive and simply walk away from the boy's physically afflicted body—his paralytic body! He then proceeded to instruct the boy to pick up his stretcher and go home. After the boy's spirit was

62. WILDFLOWERS

The Sower sows the Word, …And these are the ones on whom seed was sown on the good soil; and they hear the Word and accept it, and bear fruit, thirty, sixty, and a hundredfold. MARK 4:14,20 NAS

healed, the boy's physical body was healed. But from our perspective realize that now the boy's spirit will immediately live on into eternity, though his body will still someday be destroyed by death only later to be transformed into life and perfection. But also realize that God through the hand of Jesus did heal the paralytic's physical body. So He certainly is interested in our physical well-being and in our physical healing. So much so that He devised a plan in time to transform and unite our physical bodies with our spirits.

Remember, He is the creator of all of our physical defense mechanisms, our methods and our manners of recovering and healing. He intends for us to use them, to activate them, and to evoke them to lessen our own physical sufferings. Remember that in the beginning, He created man in perfect health. God is capable of providing and granting to individuals physical healing. To further the cause of Christ is the ultimate aim of God's interventions. He desires us to have the same aim. This potential and avenue for the restoration of health through God's healing should most certainly be sought after. Healing should be asked for through the power of prayer.

And yet the reason you don't have what you want is that you don't ask for it. And even when you do ask, you don't get it because your whole aim is wrong—you want only what will give you pleasure. JAMES 4:3 TLB

If a person's physical healing furthers the cause of man's knowledge of Christ and fits into the greater good of God's plan and Will for the individual, physical healing can certainly be accomplished.

However, if a person's illness or suffering furthers the cause of man's knowledge of Christ and fits into the greater good of God's plan and Will, He may withhold an individual's physical healing. When we receive Christ into our lives we surrender our own will and, yes, even our own life. In this Christ Himself is our example.

Your attitude should be the kind that was shown to us by Jesus Christ, who, though he was God, did not demand and cling to His rights as God, but laid aside His mighty power and glory, taking the disguise of a slave and becoming like men. And He humbled Himself even further, going so far as actually to die a criminal's death on a cross. PHILIPPIANS 2:5-8 TLB

Just as He did in Biblical times, God often calls upon the strong and courageous in spirit to give up their lives and pleasures to accomplish His plan and greater good. I have often observed what appears to be from the outside a tragic

63. FOREST FIRE

Jesus began to teach them, saying, "But, if God so arrays the grass of the field, which is alive today and tomorrow is thrown in the furnace, will He not much more do so for you...?" MATTHEW 6:30 NAS

senseless disease, injury, or death result in many persons' spiritual awakening and acceptance of Christ on the inside. In the final analysis of our lives we must faithfully surrender our person, our possessions, and our loved ones to the ultimate Will and purpose of God. In order to do so we must faithfully rely on the fulfillment of the following verse.

And we know that all that happens to us is working for our good if we love God and are fitting into His plans. ROMANS 8:28 TLB

It should also be realized that if God's healing is willed it is in His own time which is usually on a different scale than the fulfillment of our own wishes and desires. One of the most valuable assets a patient can have is patience.

Dear brothers, is your life full of difficulties and temptations? Then be happy, for when the way is rough, your patience has a chance to grow. So let it grow, and don't try to squirm out of your problems. For when your patience is finally in full bloom, then you will be ready for anything, strong in character, full and complete. JAMES 2-4 TLB

However, it should also be recognized that to accomplish and fulfill God's master plan for an individual, as it was for the very cause of Christ evidenced by his capture and crucifixion, pain and suffering may be necessary to endure.

This suffering is all part of the work God has given you. Christ, who suffered for you, is your example. I PETER 2:21

Since Christ suffered and underwent pain, you must have the same attitude He did, you must be ready to suffer, too. For remember, when your body suffers, sin loses its power and you won't be spending the rest of your life chasing after evil desires, but will be anxious to do the will of God. I PETER 4:1-2

God's reason and purpose for an individual's suffering may be for the person's greater good. In times of personal pain we are often forced to evaluate, analyze and assess our total condition in life. These thoughts often result in our reordering, restructuring, and re-prioritizing our life's goals and directions. These changes often provide an individual with the opportunity to get rid of personally harmful old habits, methods and patterns of thought and action. Simply stated, as the verse says, these personally devastating circumstances for the faithful often result in a purification of their lives. Through these situations and circumstances, the individual often becomes aware of and is able to recognize and therefore

64. WILDFLOWERS II

To every thing there is a season, and a time to every purpose under the heaven. ECCLESIASTES 3:1

resolve and discard elements of sin which may have a stronghold in his or her own life.

Even though this knowledge and recognition comes at a price of personal suffering, the eradication of personal sin always results in a more joyful, meaningful abundant life. The old potentially harmful and useless things of life give way to the opportunity for new growth and new vigor. So it is also with the unnatural world. Forest fires produce great devastation by burning and scorching the earth, but get rid of useless, non-productive undergrowth which makes way for a bounty of plentiful new life and productivity. So too it is for the believers whose endurance, tolerance, and acceptance of their own miseries are made possible by their faith in a greater good being accomplished through their own sufferings.

And we know that all that happens to us is working for our good if we love God and are fitting into His plans. ROMANS 8:28

Remember, He is an all-loving God! Take for example his ultimate desire for us:

I have come that they may have life, and have it more abundantly. MARK 10:10

For God did not send his Son into the world to condemn the world but to save the world through Him. Whoever believes in Him is not condemned, but whoever does not believe stands condemned already because he has not believed in the name of God's one and only Son. JOHN 3:17-18 NIV

He allows us to implement and facilitate our relief from misery through the activation of faith, hope, and love. He places great value on these qualities of life:

There are three things that remain: faith, hope and love—and the greatest of these is love. Let love be your greatest aim. I CORINTHIANS 14:1 TLB

Pain and suffering are a part of our unnatural life on earth. In life there is a time for all things:

To every thing there is a season, and a time to every purpose under the heaven: A time to be born, and a time to die; a time to plant, and a time to pluck up that which is planted; A time to kill, and a time to heal; a time to break down, and a time to build up; A time to weep, and a time to laugh; a time to mourn, and a time to dance; A time to cast away stones, and a time to gather stones together; a time to embrace, and a time to refrain from embracing; A time to get, and a time to lose; a time to keep, and a time to cast away; A time to rend, and a time to sew; a time to keep silence, and a time to speak; A time to love, and a time to hate; a time of war, and a time of peace.

ECCLESIASTES 3:1-8 KJV

65. DOOR

Jesus said to them again, "Yes, I AM the Door; if anyone enters through Me, he shall be saved, and shall go in and out and find pasture." JOHN 10:9 NAS

16 ◆ Prayer, Power, and Healing

Now, another dimension provided for us by which we can access God's power for healing is through prayer. Can we implement and utilize prayer as a means of obtaining physical healing?

> *Ask, and you will be given what you ask for. Seek, and you will find. Knock, and the door will be opened. For everyone who asks receives. Anyone who seeks, finds. If only you will knock, the door will be opened. If a child asks his father for a loaf of bread, will he be given a stone instead? If he asks for fish, will he be given a poisonous snake? Of course not! And if you hard-hearted, sinful men know how to give good gifts to your children, won't your Father in Heaven even more certainly give good gifts to those who ask Him for them?* MATTHEW 7:7-11 TLB

Prayer is that form of intimate communication that goes on between God and His faithful. Remember, we have a God who is all things, including a person. The Person of God is indeed interested in us as persons. In addition to managing the complex, intricate universe and all in it, He is also concerned about the personal struggles, needs, and

66. BUTTERFLY

Enter into His gate with thanksgiving and into His courts with praise. PSALM 100:4 KJV

desires of yours and mine. But how are we to pray? Who can pray? What can we ask for in prayer? How do we ask for it in prayer? Can we pray for healing?

I suppose any one person of God's creation can pray to Him. God is no respecter of persons. His Word is filled with examples of all sorts of people who pray to Him, for all sorts of reasons. But to really answer these questions about prayers since they involve knowing the Mind and Will of the Person of God we must get to know God in a personal way. Just as all of our interpersonal relationships are based on our intimate knowledge of those with whom we relate, we must also seek an intimate knowledge of our God. We must come to actually know the character of God in order to know how He thinks and what He Wills. Since God created us as individual persons, He already knows our mind, our will and our character. In order to effectively complete our side of the relationship with God we must come to know Him. We have already seen that there are two fundamental ways in which we as individuals can come to a personal knowledge of God; through our relationship and knowledge of Jesus who is God, and through our knowledge of God's Word expressed in the Bible as a revelation of His true character.

In order to know God, we must first come to personally know Him through His Son, Jesus. When we see Christ we see all of God. Remember, that is why He came to us in human form. So that we might get to know Him on our own level of human understanding. In all of the accounts of successful effective prayer in the Bible, those whose prayers were heard and answered by God had faith in Christ. In fact, in some cases even without the person voicing their request in prayer, their needs were answered by God just because He saw the evidence of their faith in Christ.

And, behold, a woman, which was diseased with an issue of blood twelve years, came behind Him, and touched the hem of His garment; For she said within herself, If I may but touch His garment, I shall be whole. But Jesus turned Him about, and when He saw her, He said, 'Daughter, be of good comfort; thy faith hath made thee whole.' And the woman was made whole from that hour.
MATTHEW 9:19-22 KJV

So I think it is reasonable to conclude that in order to improve one's chances of answered prayer a personal faith in Christ is necessary. This fundamental union is best expressed by Christ Himself in the following:

67. GRAPEVINE

I AM the true vine, and my Father is the husbandmen…I AM the vine, you are the branches…. he that abideth in Me, and I in him, the same bringeth forth much fruit: for without Me ye can do nothing."
JOHN 15:1,5 *KJV*

Yes, I AM the vine; you are the branches. Whosoever lives in Me and I in him shall produce a large crop of fruit. For apart from Me you cannot do a thing. If anyone separates from Me, he is thrown away like a useless branch, withers, and is gathered into a pile with all the others and burned. But if you stay in Me and obey My commands, you may ask any request you like and it will be granted! My true disciples produce bountiful harvest. This brings glory to my father. JOHN 15:5-8 TLB

The chance of our prayers being answered are increased, if they align with the Will and Intent of God, and as seen in the previous verse, if we are obedient to His Word. This does require not only a recognition on our part, of our tendency toward sin, and our subsequent need for forgiveness, but also requires our willful intent to turn from our sins through repentance. Asking for forgiveness from our sins is *talking the walk*. Repentance from our sins demands the action of *walking the talk*. Although, there are times when a respectful insistent and determined prayer can result in God actually changing His Mind and Will in a certain situation. Such was the case when the people living in the city of Nineveh turned from their sinful ways. God saved their city. Jonah was sent to Nineveh to tell them of their impending destruction. When the residents of the city heard of their coming destruction, they believed Jonah, and turned from their ungodly ways. They began to seek God's forgiveness and repented from their sinful ways. Their prayers were heard by God and as a result their city was saved from sure destruction.

And when God saw that they had put a stop to their evil ways He abandoned His plan to destroy them and didn't carry it through. JONAH 3:10 TLB

So, the people of Nineveh were saved. Not merely as a result of their prayers, but as a result of their repentance from their sins and a faith and a belief in the absolute authority of their God. Such interactions and interplay of events, thoughts, desires and actions are possible in our own lives today.

Now, in order to assure our success at prayer in our lives, are we alone or do we have a mechanism for help? The whole mechanism of prayer is presented in the Bible as a picture of the workings between the personal believer, Jesus the Son, God the Father, and the Third Person of God, the Holy Spirit. You see, after a person receives Christ, he is indwelt with the Holy Spirit. Yes, the person of God who actually takes up residence in the believer is the Holy Spirit. Our original human spirit when combined with God through Jesus becomes the complete Spirit of God in us as the Holy Spirit. It is the Holy Spirit who guides us from the inside into our personal dealings with God. It is the Holy Spirit who actually prays from us and for us and for our personal desires and needs to God the Father. Even when we don't know what to pray for the Holy Spirit silently conveys to God our prayerful petition.

And in the same way—by our faith—the Holy Spirit helps us with our daily problems and in our praying. For we don't even know what we should pray for, nor how to pray as we should; but the Holy Spirit prays for us with such feeling that it cannot be expressed in words. And the Father who knows all hearts knows, of course what the Spirit is saying as He pleads for us in harmony with God's own Will. And we know that all that happens to us is working for our good if we love God and are fitting into His plans. ROMANS 8: 26-28 TLB

The true task for us as believers is to surrender our will, intent, and thoughts to those of the Holy Spirit and of God. To align our will with the Will of God. The chance of our prayers being answered are increased if they align with the Will of God. And we now have three individual and personal tutors to teach us the Will of God—our relationship with the Son, Jesus, our study in understanding of the Word and the silent supernatural direction from the Holy Spirit.

This hope we have as an anchor of the soul, a hope both sure and steadfast, and one which enters within the veil where Jesus has entered as a forerunner for us, having become a High Priest forever according to the order of Melchizedek. HEBREWS 6:19-20 NAS

When Jesus fulfilled His mission of life, death, and resurrection He left His believers with the presence of the Holy Spirit. In His personal absence He knew His followers and believers would be shaken in faith and strength. So He told them not to fear, that the Holy Spirit would indwell them and would be the One who in His absence would lead them into all truth; and that the Holy Spirit would enable them to do greater things than ever before.

If you love Me, obey Me. And I will ask the Father and He will give you another comforter, and He will never leave you. He is the Holy Spirit, the Spirit who leads into all truth. The world at large cannot receive Him, for it isn't looking for Him and doesn't recognize Him.

But you do, for He lives with you now and some day shall be in you. No, I will not abandon you or leave you as orphans in the storm— I will come to you. In just a little while I will be gone from the world, but I will still be present with you. JOHN 14:15-19 TLB

But when the Father sends the comforter instead of Me—and by the comforter I mean the Holy Spirit—He will teach you much, as well as remind you of everything I Myself have told you. JOHN 14:26 TLB

While the Holy Spirit is directing our thoughts, desires, and will from the inside, Jesus is our advocate before the Father in Heaven. There is no other advocate, intermediary, or mediator between us and God, except Jesus.

Jesus reassured His believers and us even more by teaching that after His return to Heaven He would be before the Father as our personal advocate. That since He lived here as a human, He knew first hand the degree and extent of our needs, desires, and sufferings. And with that personal knowledge of experience, as is ours, He would plead our case before the Father in Heaven. This reassuring promise is clearly stated in the following:

My little children, I am telling you this so that you will stay away from sin. But if you sin, there is someone to plead for you before the Father. His name is Jesus Christ, the One who is all that is good and who pleases God completely. He is the One who took God's wrath against our sins upon Himself, and brought us into fellowship with God; and he is the forgiveness of our sins, and not only ours but all the world's. I JOHN 2:1-2 TLB

There seems to be another simple condition in activating this mechanism of prayer. It greatly pleases God, establishes the believer's faith in Christ and activates the advocacy of Jesus before God if the prayer is offered in Jesus' name.

You can ask Him for anything, using My Name, and I will do it, for this will bring praise to the Father because of what I, the Son, will do for you. Yes, ask anything, using My Name, and I will do it! JOHN 14:13-14 TLB

So, we have before us a very reassuring system of prayer and communication with our personal God. A form of communication called prayer, derived from the guidance of the Holy Spirit from within, based upon God's Will in the Bible, offered in the name of our Lord and Savior, Jesus, and taken directly to God by our

68. PATH

Jesus told him, "I AM the Way—yes, and the Truth and the Life. No one can get to the Father except by means of Me." JOHN 14:6 TLB

advocate in Heaven, Jesus. We have the added assurance that our prayers are strengthened and fortified by the faithful prayers of our families, friends, and fellow believers.

We have seen in previous examples that the power of God is that power of life itself which resides in all of His creation. But we have evidence that the power of God actually works outside of our physical selves in a supernatural way enlisted through prayer. In other words, does prayer really work and can prayer effectively alter the course of our lives and the course of our diseases and illnesses? Can the power of the faithful really affect those things, circumstances, situations, and persons on the outside?

A recent medical study conducted by Dr. Randolph Byrd at San Francisco General Hospital documents the effects of prayer on a group of patients admitted to an intensive care unit. The prayer group was made up of a group of professing christians who prayed to the Judeo-Christian God in Heaven in the name of His Son, Jesus. The patients were unaware of the fact that a prayer team was actually praying for their health and recovery. This fact is very important! Since they were unaware of the prayer being offered on their behalf, it's affects could not have been mediated through the patients' own mind, but from an outside supernatural power. An equal number of patients were used as a control group who did not have the advantage of the power of prayer in their behalf. At the end of the study, the patients whose care included prayers had fewer medical complications, fewer mechanical medical interventions, and in fact fewer died in comparison to the group of patients without prayer. There is indeed within the construction of scientific investigation and thought evidence to support the existence of the supernatural power of God called into action by the prayers of His faithful believers on behalf of His suffering children.

So, it appears that an individual's human spirit, when united and joined with the Spirit of God through Christ, enables us to implement the personal supernatural power of an unlimited and boundless God. The implementation of this supernatural power can literally create healing of body, soul and spirit. This supernatural power enables God's faithful believers to not only have an impact on their own healing and circumstance, but also impact all of those things, machines, technology, circumstance and even other people around them.

69. SUNRISE

Now glory be to God who by His mighty power at work within us is able to do far more than we would ever dare to ask or even dream of—intimately beyond our highest prayers, desires, thoughts or hopes.
EPHESIANS 3:17-20 TLB

As you personally contemplate and apply the power of prayer in your circumstance I would offer up this prayer in your behalf:

"And I pray that Christ will be more and more at home in your hearts, living within you as you trust in Him. May your roots go down deep into the soil of God's marvelous love and may you be able to feel and understand as all God's children should, how long, how wide, how deep and how high His love really is; and to experience this love for yourselves, though it is so great that you will never see the end of it or fully know or understand it. And so at last, you will be filled up with God Himself."

Now glory be to God who by His mighty power at work within us is able to do far more than we would ever dare to ask or even dream of— intimately beyond our highest prayers, desires, thoughts, or hopes. EPHESIANS 3:17-20 TLB

I hope you will be filled with the power and presence of our personal God to accomplish great things. But to be filled, as I personally found, one at times first has to experience emptiness. In order to really experience the completeness and fullness of the Power of God in your own life, and in your state of need, you must draw your personal line in the sand and give your heart and soul to God in order to experience the fullness and richness of His Grace, Love, and Blessings.

In my great trouble, I cried to the Lord and He answered me; from the depths of death I called, and Lord, You heard me!...

I sank beneath the waves and death was very near. The waters closed above me, the seaweed wrapped itself around my head. I went down to the bottoms of the mountains that rise from off the ocean floor. I was locked out of life and imprisoned in the land of death. But, O Lord, my God, You have snatched me from the yawning jaws of death!

When I had lost all hope, I turned my thoughts once more to the Lord, and my earnest prayer went to You in Your Holy Temple.

I will never worship anyone but You! For how can I thank You enough for all You have done? I will surely fulfill my promises. For my deliverance comes from the Lord alone. JONAH 2:2-9

In the above verse, Jonah very well articulates the gratitude, thankfulness and faithfulness for those of us who have been overcome by turbulent waters, lost all hope, but whose prayers were answered.

70. Nest-Building for Winter

Now just as you trusted Christ to save you, trust Him, too, for each day's problems; live in vital union with Him. Colossians 2:6 TLB

17 • My Hope and Prayers for You

I hope that your life will be characterized by peace of mind, contentment and a reassuring sense of meaning and purpose. I hope that your relationships will not be characterized by strife, anger, resentment, and guilt; but be characterized by love, forgiveness, kindness and loyalty. When life presents you with an obstacle, a conflict, a tragedy, or a period of suffering, I hope that in the midst of your personal agony, you will see the hand of God at work in the construction of your person. I hope that during periods of individual strife and trouble, you are able to activate the powers energized by faith, hope, and love which will be able to see you through the circumstance.

And that most importantly you have the faith to be able to surrender your will to the Will of God. That when heartache and sorrow are the unnatural pains of a circumstance or situation you have the faith to look past your own feelings and realize that the ultimate Will of God is being done. That your personal sacrifice and suffering is accomplishing a greater good than you may be able to see.

71. LANDSCAPE

And God said unto Moses, "I AM THAT I AM…" EXODUS 3:14 KJV

And Jesus said unto them, "Verily, verily, I say unto you, Before Abraham was, I AM." JOHN 8:58 KJV

I hope that you have the faith to accept God's answers to your prayers. That your faith accepts the ultimate authority of God for all things in your life. Then you will have gained the position of realizing the fruits of the Holy Spirit:

But when the Holy Spirit controls our lives, He will produce this kind of fruit in us: love, joy, peace, patience, kindness, goodness, faithfulness, gentleness and self control. GALATIANS 5:22-23

In this position there is no risk, insecurity, stress or strife. Just experience the reality and security of Romans 8:28:

And we know that all that happens to us is working for our good and are fitting into His plans.

In the final evaluation of our lives and our situations and circumstances, we as persons, individuals, and humans have little control. God who created our universe and all things in it is the ultimate authority. Our individual trials, triumphs and tragedies are under His control. Whether we experience pain, suffering, and loss, or health, wellness, and life, God's Will will be done. He will give to us that which is for our best good and that which brings others to know Christ. Our attitude should not be one of demanding our own

will, although, a Christian does have the right and privilege to ask God for the granting his own will. But we should most importantly be willing and able to relinquish our own personal desires and will to that of accepting God's Will. In this, Christ again should be our example:

Your attitude should be the kind that was shown us by Jesus Christ, who, though He was God, did not demand and cling to His rights as God, but laid aside His mighty power and glory, taking the disguise of a slave, and becoming like men. And He humbled Himself even further, going so far as actually to die a criminal's death on a cross. PHILIPPIANS 2:5-8 TLB

After all, as the Master not only of our individual lives, but as the Master of the entire multiply complex and intricate universe, He knows best. Remember, He knows all things that we can see, but even more profound those things that we can't see. So what looks one way to us may look entirely different to Him.

For example the desire of our heart and our will on a scorching hot afternoon may be to soak in a pleasant, cool, refreshing pool of water. But for some reason, our desires are not granted. We get mad and angry and throw a fit of rage because we can see nothing but good for ourselves

72. Dad Feeding Baby Robins

Jesus began to teach them, saying, "Look at the birds! They don't worry about what to eat—they don't need to sow or reap or store up food—for your heavenly Father feeds them. And you are far more valuable to Him than they are." Matthew 6:26

basking in this cool, calm, fresh water on a hot day. But our desires are rejected and our plans are thwarted by God! Why?

Because below the surface of the calm cool pool of water lay the deadly Ebola virus, poisonous snakes, and alligators. God sees everything and the depths of all situations and circumstances. His Will may divert us from what we think should have been, could have been, and according to us, would have been, but His Will is always what is best for us.

In fact, recent studies evaluating the success of prayers demonstrates that the most pointed, demanding and direct prayers for one's own will to be enforced were not the most effectively answered. The most effective manner in which to ask God for something is not to ask in a demanding way. Ask specifically, but ask with an attitude that you are fully submitting to God's ultimate authority and Will regarding any answer as His best answer. Boy, that takes Faith! I came to this knowledge at my son's bedside when he was the most critically ill. Oh, how I wanted him to live! But oh, how little control I had in the final decision.

When I acknowledged in brokenness and emptiness my personal weaknesses, my failures, and my shortcomings, and was led into an attitude of submission, I relinquished my will to God's Will. At that hour and in that circumstance, God's Will was for Brad to live. That is the only reason, he, or I, or you live at this moment and in this time. Some are required to give up a loved one. The depth of their pain I can only imagine. The strength of their faith must be enormous. By comparison, I cannot boast of the strength or endurance of their faith. And, remember, that which God regards over all else is faith. What is faith? There is a biblical definition for faith:

> *What is faith? It is the confident assurance that something we want is going to happen. It is the certainty that what we hope for is waiting for us, even though we cannot see it up ahead. Men of God in days of old were famous for their faith. By faith—by believing God—we know that the world and the stars—in fact, all things—were made at God's command; and that they were all made from things that can't be seen.* HEBREWS 11:1-3 TLB

To those brave, faithful individuals goes my admiration. But to God goes the glory because He too has given them faith as a free gift.

No matter the size of the issue, dilemma, situation or circumstance, the Person of God

73. Baby Robins

Jesus began saying to His disciples first of all, "What is the price of five sparrows? A couple of pennies? Not much more than that, yet God does not forget a single one of them. And he knows the number of hairs on your head! Never fear, you are far more valuable to Him than a flock of sparrows." LUKE 12:6-7 *TLB*

through Christ is sufficient. It is Him and only Him in us that makes us as individuals sufficient. His provision for you and me is complete. Take as an example, the cares and provisions for the simple little sparrow. From one moment to the next does the sparrow fret and worry over his next meal? No, in the very next tree, on the sidewalk, in the street, in the next barn yard, or at the next feeder will be his next meal. His provision is there—no need to expend time, effort, and energy in fear or fret—it is just there! Just as God's provision is spontaneous, perpetual and ever-present for the simple sparrow so it is there for you and I. His provision is as spontaneous and as effortless as your next heart beat. After all, how hard do you have to struggle or work to ensure that your heart beats? That mechanism of life is just there. So too, is God's total provision for not only your body, but also your soul and your eternal spirit. If His provision is so complete for one of his natural creatures, how much more so should it be complete for you and I who are like him and joined to him in spirit through His Son, Christ.

So, here you have it! In clear view for the seeing. The nature of God is to make provision for his creation—from sparrows to mankind—for you and for me.

What is the price of five sparrows? A couple of pennies? Not much more than that, yet God does not forget a single one of them. And he knows the number of hairs on your head! Never fear, you are far more valuable to Him than a flock of sparrows. LUKE 12:6-7 TLB

Remember, that after receiving the true gift of Christ when God looks upon you, He no longer sees the elements and attributes imparted to you by the unnatural world. He only sees the presence and characteristics of His Son. When He looks at you, He sees Jesus. Does that make you worth anything? The Master of the entire universe, the creator of all nature and all life, values you so greatly He died for you! What does that make you worth? You are worth everything to Him!

He died so that you may live and live with these promises for your life. The Bible has over eight hundred promises for the believer.

The steps of good men are directed by the Lord. He delights in each step they take. If they fall it isn't fatal, for the Lord holds them with His hand. I have been young and now I am old. And in all my years I have never seen the Lord forsake a man who loves Him; nor have I seen the children of the godly go hungry. Instead, the

74. EAGLE

But they that wait upon the Lord shall renew their strength; they shall mount up with wings as eagles; they shall run and not be weary; and they shall walk, and not faint. ISAIAH 40:31 *KJV*

godly are able to be generous with their gifts and loans to others, and their children are a blessing. PSALM 37:23-26 TLB

Don't be impatient for the Lord to act! Keep traveling steadily along His pathway and in due season He will honor you with every blessing, and you will see the wicked destroyed. I myself have seen it happen; a proud and evil man, towering like a cedar of Lebanon, but when I looked again, he was gone! I searched but could not find him! But the good man— what a different story! For the good man—the blameless, the upright, the man of peace—he has a wonderful future ahead of him. For him there is a happy ending. But evil men shall be destroyed, and their posterity shall be cut off. The Lord saves the godly! He is their salvation and their refuge when trouble comes. Because they trust in Him, He helps them and delivers them from the plots of evil men. PSALM 37:34-40 TLB

I have observed the truth of these promises to be realized in the lives of God's faithful. More importantly, to my own faith, I have experienced the fruition of these promises in my own life. I have faith that you who receive Christ, commit to follow Him and love Him, will experience the same provisions from God's promises.

His faithful will also be sustained and lifted up as individuals:

But they that wait upon the Lord shall renew their strength; they shall mount up with wings as eagles; they shall run and not be weary; and they shall walk, and not faint. ISAIAH 40:31 KJV

So too, will nations built upon a foundation of faith in Jesus, and adherent to an inerrant world of God, be sustained and uplifted. In our arrogance, we often conclude that our success and dominance can be attributed to our own inherent resources and attributes as a people, when in fact our many successes and triumphs, both as individuals and as a nation, are blessings bestowed upon us by God.

Blessed is the nation whose God is the Lord, Whose people He has chosen as His own. PSALM 33:12 TLB

Our continued success is based not on our own attributes as a people, but rather on the object of our beliefs and faith. For us to continue to succeed as a nation and as individuals we must awaken to and commit ourselves to faith in God through Christ, and adopt as our individual and national conscience the following of the absolute truth as revealed to us in the Holy Scriptures. This is a sentiment voiced by one of our nation's most profound leaders.

It is the duty of nations as well as men to owe their dependence upon the overruling Power of God—and to recognize the sublime truth answered in the Holy Scriptures and proved by all history, that those nations only are blessed where God is the Lord.

–Abraham Lincoln

May God richly bless you!
    A sinner saved by faith in God's grace,
    Mark Paul Bishop M.D.

REFERENCES

Benson, Herbert M.D. *The Mind Body Effect.* New York: Simon and Schuster, 1979.

Bliss, Richard B. *Origins: Creation or Evolution.* El Cajon CA: Institute for Creation Research, 1984.

Byrd, Randolph C. M.D. "Positive Therapeutic Effects of Intercessory Prayer in a Coronary Care Unit Population." *Southern Medical Journal.* Vol 81, July 1988, p 826.

Davis, Paul. *God and the New Physics.* New York: Simon and Schuster, 1983.

Dobson, James. *Dare to Discipline.* Wheaton IL: Tyndale House, 1970.

…*The Strong Willed Child.* Wheaton IL: Tyndale House.

Graham, Billy. *How to Be Born Again.* Waco TX: Word Books.

…*The Holy Spirit.* Waco TX: Word Books, 1978.

Goldman, Daniel. *Emotional Intelligence.* New York: Bantam, 1995.

Hawking, Stephen. *A Brief HIstory of Time.* New York: Bantam, 1988.

Jahn, Robert G., and Brenda J. Duppe. *Margins of Reality.* San Diego: Harcourt, Brace, Jovanovich, 1983.

Janis, Irving L. *Current Trends in Psychology, Readings from American Scientist.* Los Altos CA: William Kaufman, 1977.

Lindsey, Hal. *There's A New World Coming.* Eugene OR: Harvest House, 1973.

McDowell, Josh. *Evidence that Demands a Verdict.* [city]: Campus Crusade for Christ, 1972.

…and Don Stewart. *Handbook of Today's Religions.* Nashville: Thomas Nelson, 1992.

…*Answers to Tough Questions Skeptics Ask About the Christian Faith.* Wheaton IL: Tyndale House, 1980.

Meier, Paul D. *Christian Child-Rearing and Personality Development.* Grand Rapids MI: Baker Book House, 1977.

…and Frank Minerth. *Happiness Is a Choice.* Grand Rapids MI: Baker Book House, 1978.

Middleton, William S. *Values in Modern Medicine.* Madison WI: University of Wisconsin Press, 1972.

Morris, Henry M. *The Genesis Record.* Grand Rapids MI: Baker Book House, 1976.

…*The Revelation Record.* Grand Rapids MI: Baker Book House, 1983.

…*Scientific Creationism.* Green Forest AR: Master Books, 1974.

Nee, Watchman. *The Return of the Spirit.* Fort Washington PA: Christian Literature Crusade, 1977.

…*Sit, Walk and Stand.* Fort Washington PA: Christian Literature Crusade, 1980.

…*The Spiritual Man.* Fort Washington PA: Christian Literature Crusade, 1977.

Zimbargo, Phillip G. and Floyd L. Ruck. *Psychology and Life.* Glenview IL: Scott Foresman, 1977.

ABOUT THE
AUTHOR/PHOTOGRAPHER

[Reprinted with permission from *Wisconsin State Journal,* Madison, Wisconsin, September 3, 1996.]

The good doctor
Top physician relies on humor, caring and inner strength
by Dee J. Hall
Photos by Roger Turner

DODGEVILLE — This is the story of Dr. Mark Bishop, a successful small-town doctor who graduated near the top of his UW-Madison medical school class.

Handsome and upbeat, Bishop is married to a strong, supportive wife, Judy. When not busy raising three high-achieving children, Bishop, who practices in Dodgeville and Mineral Point, finds time to take professional-quality photos and write inspirational books.

Last month, surrounded by the warmth of his family and the accolades of his colleagues, Bishop was named Wisconsin's Family Physician of the Year.

He's the kind of guy you might be tempted to hate because his life seems so perfect.

But appearances can be tricky: Bishop actually has faced, and overcome, some of the most difficult times a person can. That is why, perhaps, the boy who grew up the son of a Sauk Prairie doctor makes such a good doctor himself.

Eight years ago, Bishop's son, Brad, was diagnosed with leukemia, launching a three-year round of chemotherapy that nearly killed him. During that time,

Bishop admits that the needs of his other children, Carrie and Brent, were virtually ignored.

Because of Brad's illness, Bishop put off surgery needed to correct his own spinal cord injury caused when he was bucked off a horse three years earlier.

"I just doubled my pain pills and kept trudging along," Bishop said.

It took 23 hours of surgeries and six months in a body cast to repair the physical damage, but his addiction to painkillers remained.

"I could never reduce the dose," Bishop said. "I just couldn't find it within myself to recover once again."

In 1989, Bishop took part in a program run by the Medical Society of Wisconsin to help physicians overcome drug and alcohol problems. Although "humiliated" by having to admit his addiction, Bishop kicked the habit after a month-long stay at a treatment center.

And Brad—despite a harrowing series of complications including strokes, blood clots in his brain, kidney failure, temporary blindness and nearly choking to death—beat his cancer and is now an honors student at UW-Platteville. The leukemia is unlikely to recur, Bishop said.

It was only through the strength of his wife, Judy, a hair stylist, and their spiritual faith, that the Bishop family stayed together, he said.

"Our whole family became dysfunctional," Bishop said in the lounge of the Memorial Hospital of Iowa County in Dodgeville. "We were scared and hurt and distraught.

"When you get shaken to the

rafters by this type of series of events, you look for something to hang your hat on. We held on to our faith."

Bishop also has struggled with what he now believes is a learning disability. The son of Dr. Paul and Alice Bishop, he graduated in the bottom 25 percent of his Sauk Prairie High School class and was urged by a counselor to forego college.

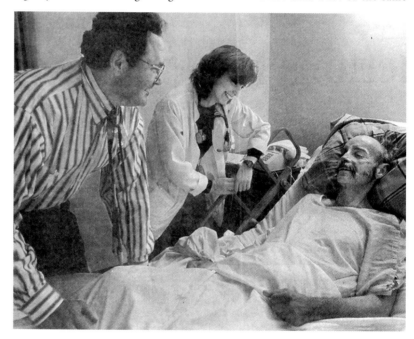

But Bishop decided to take a year to "grow up," then apply himself in college. Bishop started to excel after he figured out that the only way for him to remember something was to hear it out loud. Years of reading to himself quietly in the corner of the Chemistry Building Library culminated in Bishop's induction

into the Alpha Omega Alpha Honor Medical Society.

Bishop said he got through those tough years – and helps patients with their own trials – with tools he discovered outside the classroom. They are faith, hope and love and – almost above all – humor.

"Humor does a lot of the same things, physiologically, that faith, hope and love do," said Bishop, 50, who often gives talks on the value of a good laugh.

That includes being able to poke fun at his own misfortunes. Recalling a particularly grim Christmas when he and Brad were sick, Bishop says with a chuckle, "I was in one hospital bed in

Bishop has written and illustrated a 45-page inspirational book using his own photographs. Here he shows a portrait of one of his late patients, 96-year-old Otto Tesh. "He's one of those special relationships you develop as a doctor. I used to go check on him at his house. He didn't like coming to the doctor. But he lived all alone. I worried about him a lot."

the living room and he (Brad) was in the other. We looked like a M*A*S*H unit."

Last month as he made rounds at Memorial Hospital, Bishop took time to laugh with patient Gene Cox of Mineral Point, who apparently thought Bishop was kidding when he warned that a newspaper photographer and reporter

would be tagging along.

"I guess I play a lot of practical jokes around here..." Bishop said, trying to explain the surprised look on Cox's face.

Cox came to Bishop in late June with complaints of heartburn. His wife, Bonnie, said they thought it was an ulcer. But Gene Cox has a rare, and fast-moving, form of stomach cancer. His outlook, admits Bonnie Cox, is "not good."

Through it all, Cox said, they've been grateful to have Bishop at their side.

"I can't praise him enough," she said. "He has a super, super bedside manner. He takes you as an individual. You don't feel like a number, like in some places. He just sits there until you're done talking.

"He's just an excellent doctor. We're very, very fortunate to have him in our community."

Such testimonials prompted the Wisconsin Academy of Family Physicians in mid-August to give Bishop it's highest honor.

After Bishop was nominated, he was asked to provide letters of support from co-workers and patients. Nearly two dozen poured in, said Dawn Maerker, administrative assistant for the academy, which is based in Elm Grove.

"He works well with nursing personnel, listening to their observations and concerns," Maerker said, reading from one letter.

"The seniors love him. He gets his patients to laugh," said another. "He has

time for his patients...(and) cares for their emotional and spiritual needs," said another letter.

For all of medicine's advances, Bishop says that sometimes, "the warmth of a caressing hand," is the best medicine. That's when Bishop orders up the "Hanson procedure" for his patients, a soothing backrub administered by Mary Hanson, a nurse's aide at Memorial.

And while some physicians remain detached as a way of coping with their stressful jobs, Bishop believes in being closely involved.

"If I've got someone taking care of me, I want more than someone who will share their scientific expertise with me but also share their heart and their mind," Bishop said.

"In a small town," he adds, "your patients are also your neighbors. You see them in the grocery store. You see them at the football games. They're part of your life. That's why it's hard to be detached from them."

In essence, Bishop is the type of doctor the medical profession needs more of, said John Frey, chairman of the department of family medicine at the UW-Madison School of Medicine. The United States needs more family doctors, Frey said, especially in its rural areas and inner cities.

"The good thing about Dr. Bishop is not only is he a family doctor...but he's also practicing in a community that needs him," Frey said.

[Reprinted with permission from *The Democrat Tribune,* The City of Mineral Point, Wisconsin, August 22, 1996.]

Proud to know Dr. Bishop: "Family Physician of the Year"

by Jeanie Lewis

The gift of life is precious to Dr. Mark Bishop, recently named "Family Physician of the Year" at ceremonies this past Saturday at the annual Scientific Assembly held at the Grand Geneva Resort in Lake Geneva. Not just because he is a physician and it's his profession, but because of personal experience he shares: "I am one who has learned to be thankful just to be alive and well, and to greet each new day with gratitude and enthusiasm." Dr. Bishop was referring to a time in his own life when circumstances granted him a full view of the medical equation—both as a physician and as a patient.

Dr. Bishop suffered through the pain, disability and dysfunction of a spinal cord injury. The Bishop family accompanied by a brother "through frustrating, unfair and senseless sufferings of a chronic mental illness." Then there was son Brad's gallant battle and ultimate victory over acute lymphoblastic leukemia attended by multiple complications. Not only was the sickness devastating, but also Bishop felt guilt for not being able to provide his other two children, Brent and Carrie, a normal struc-

ture in their lives. He'd also become dependent on pain medication.

In the aftermath of these devastating circumstances, Dr. Bishop acknowledges: "I found myself and my family physically, emotionally, mentally and spiritually bankrupt. High tech medicine had repaired his spine and healed Brad's bone marrow, but in the wake of their physical sufferings, Dr. Bishop said, "our minds, hearts, souls and spirits were left broken and shattered."

To compound all of this, he faced the fears of public humiliation and personal and professional condemnation when admitting himself to the State Medical Society's Impaired Physician Program for rehabilitation. From being an honor student (as he had been in both medical school and college), a respected physician's standpoint came the realization "does an M.D. degree immunize one against the forces of nature, and the natural human weaknesses and afflictions encountered by others?" The answer was apparent to Bishop, NO!

Some may call this a rude awakening, but Dr. Bishop who has a strong faith in God, feels thee events were not "mere chance circumstances." For him, both the personal pain encountered and the personal knowledge acquired had been too great not to serve a purpose. He quotes Friedrick vonSchiller: "There is no such thing as chance, and what we regard as blind circumstance actually stems from the deepest source of all."

"All of a sudden I realized the tremendous courage, strength, fortitude, faith and perseverance my patients had

demonstrated as I had seen so many overcome similar obstacles to defy the odds of dysfunction and disability and even death," he adds.

He also realized how an illness in a family member metastasizes to the entire family. "It wasn't until my own misery and state of dependence could I identify with the pain, fear, and distressful uncertainty of being a patient. Nor could I fully appreciate both the responsibility and the unlimited opportunity a physician has to intervene, influence, improve and salvage individual human lives and entire human families. The opportunity to exhaust one's human potential as well as the depth and breadth of academic knowledge, technical skill, or personal commitment offered for consumption in the service to others through practicing medicine has no endpoint, according to Dr. Bishop.

He continued, "My reverent gratitude is to my patients whose lives have been opened and laid bare before me for my inspection and at times to my invasion. To be entrusted with the life of another is the greatest personal privilege and honor that can be given to anyone."

He said that almost daily he reminds himself of why he wants to be a physician: At age eight he already knew that he wanted "my life to make a difference in this world." Watching his father Paul, a physician, made him realize the great importance doctors are in the lives of people." On his medical school application the question was asked, "Why do yo want to be a physician?" Dr. Bishop answered: "I want to exhaust my human potential in the service of my fellow man." His thoughts remain basically the same but today he has the added assurance of experience.

While Dr. Bishop is appreciative of the superlative words of congratulations, he prepared a 21-page speech that talked namely of faith, hope and love between doctors and their patients. He said that while mastery of science and technology is important, "caring" for the patient should be the ultimate goal.

In his own special way of making a point, Bishop recalled a patient who as his condition worsened had been forced to leave his care by the patients' HMO in order to qualify as a liver transplant. Visiting later, Bishop applauded the nearly incomprehensive science and technology which was responsible for the man's organ transplant and survival. However, the man halted the accolades of scientific technology and skill of doctors to say: "I don't want to seem ungrateful, but your profession has a problem. The structure to which I surrendered my life

is unfriendly, unkind, arrogant, rude, uncaring, self-serving, and at times even hostile. My perception is that it is also greedy." The man offered a prescription as well: "What a person needs going through this maze of science, technology and super specialists is an advocate. Unfortunately in spite of all of the capable and qualified physicians I encountered, not one had become my personal advocate."

Standing before his colleagues, many of whom hold high offices and esteem in their profession, Bishop noted the divisions of their profession. He pointed to "gratitude toward our science" on one hand but criticism toward the display of "our art" on the other. He noted, "in all honesty to myself, I have been an accomplice in committing these violations also."

"Contributing to the erosion of our patients' trust, confidence and faith is corporate medicines' mind set of buyouts, paybacks, gag rules, lack of referral bonuses, and a diagnostic mentality of less is best. What perceptions are our patients to have of us? Is it any wonder that our patients are often angry, fearful, confused and skeptical of our actions and motivations? When the bond of trust, confidence, and faith between us and our patients is broken our most potent therapeutic tool is lost," Bishop stressed.

He contends that the very nature of family physicians affords them the best opportunity to mend the doctor-patient relationship. "The scientific disciplines have always recognized the universal prominence of love and its place of residence in the human soul," Dr. Bishop

said. The form and substance of this love upon which the most beneficial and effective human relationships and human activities are based, Dr. Bishop quoted: John 4:8: "God is love."

He challenged the physicians to take the mastery of three works to the patient's bedside: the textbook of medicine for which he gains a command of the science; the works of Shakespeare from which he gains understanding of human nature; and the Holy Bible from which he gains a perspective of the human soul and spirit.

Bishop noted that with the addition of God into the therapeutic equation, there is also generated the products of faith and hope, and he quoted I Corinthians 13:13: "There are three things that remain; faith, hope and love." Referring to this 2,000-year-old message to mankind, Dr. Bishop noted the foundational precept to be deeply rooted in the origins of medicine.

"Medicine is an art, not a trade, a calling, not a business, a calling in which the heart will be exercised equally with the head." Dr. Bishop quoted Sir William Osler, "Ours is a responsibility to unite the time-honored art of caring for the soul and spirit through the engagement of our God and our own person; while implementing the highest level of scientific technology through the application of our knowledge and understanding of the human body," he added.

"Preoccupation with the bounties of the scientific revolution have diverted energies and emphasis away from the mastery of the art," Bishop said. "This diversion has led to the decline and erosion of the doctor-patient relationship. May we see that relationships are both bonds of the heart, soul and spirit, and of the mind and intellect. This development is necessary for the investment of ourselves into the mastery of our art. Our God is both the author and the engineer of human interpersonal relationships," he stressed.

Dr. Bishop noted that many physicians have banished God from the sickroom, largely because they've banished Him from their personal lives. "Let us humble ourselves before His presence and ask Him into our own lives," he added. "In so doing, enabling us to assume our rightful position in medicine as our patients' diligent, trusted, loyal, and yes, loving advocates."

Dr. Bishop added a hope and a prayer for the 21st century physician: "For honesty over deceit, humility over arrogance, kindness over rudeness, understanding over confusion, compassion over indifference, advocacy over passivity, faith over the darkness of uncertainty, hope over the odds of defeat, and most importantly, love over all."

He added that the intangible factors and derivatives of faith, hope and love will often compel the patient onward and forward during his times of lonely, fearful and painful combat with disease. Dr. Bishop suggested that these "intangible forces may be a vital, yes, a determining factor, in life and death."

Dr. Bishop said, "aspiring to regain the honored physicians stature is not an impossible but an imperative mission." He directed them to Galatians 5:14: "For the law can be summed up in this one command, Love others as you would yourself."

He saluted the doctors, calling them "foot soldiers in the war, willing to devote their lives to the often unglamorous trenches of the front lines of the battle for human success and survival over affliction, pain and disease."

Dr. Bishop noted, "And with equal admiration, I salute our families who unselfishly give us to our calling. Our spouses (Judy) and children are truly those who are the wind beneath our wings..." At the conclusion of his speech, Dr. Bishop was given a standing ovation by his peers, family and friends.

Dr. James Jones, President of the National Academy of Family Physicians, remarked: "I feel proud to be in a room with THE Dr. Mark Bishop – Family Physician of the Year."